"It is not the critic who counts; not the man who points out how the strong man stumbles, or where the doer of deeds could have done them better. The credit belongs to the man who is actually in the arena, whose face is marred by dust and sweat and blood; who strives valiantly; who errs, who comes short again and again, because there is no effort without error and shortcoming; but who does actually strive to do the deeds; who knows great enthusiasms, the great devotions; who spends himself in a worthy cause; who at the best knows in the end the triumph of high achievement, and who at the worst, if he fails, at least fails while daring greatly, so that his place shall never be with those cold and timid souls who neither know victory nor defeat."

- Theodore Roosevelt

To the sport of wrestling that demanded so much but gave back so much more. It took blood, sweat and tears, but gave back confidence, character and valuable life lessons which could have only been gained from toeing the line.

Dedicated to my parents and grandparents who always supported and encouraged me to strive for excellence in all that I did. I could not have achieved my goals without your love and support.

To my father who never missed a match and exemplified the meaning of hard work and dedication. Thank you for pushing me beyond my comfort zone and for leading by example. You invested your time, your money, your patience and so much more to help me chase my dreams. I am forever grateful and I am thankful to call you Dad.

To my past teammates, coaches, family and friends that helped me every day to get where I wanted to be. Thank you for impacting my life in a positive way.

To my pastors and teachers who encouraged me, taught me and grounded me in the Truth. Thank you for sharing God's Word with me and for encouraging me in my daily walk.

To my brother, Matt, and my sister, Ashley, who endured growing up with long weekends in a gym and even longer wrestling seasons. Thank you both for your support. I know it was not always easy.

To my little brother, Colton, who left this earth way too soon. You are missed everyday. I look forward to seeing you again. One Love Brother.

To my three children, Branson, Addison and Ava. You are my greatest blessings and lasting legacy. I am so thankful for each of you. You are each unique and extraordinary. You can accomplish anything you set your minds to. Believe in yourselves and trust God always. I love each of you so much.

To my wife, Susie, who stood by my side and loved and supported me through it all. Thank you for your love, your grace and your unwaivering faith. It is a privilege to share this life with you.

Thank you all and God bless.

ROYCE EYER

DIVISION III NATIONAL CHAMPION

ROYCE EYER

- 2001 Lycoming College 157lb Division III Wrestling National Champion
- 2x Lycoming College Division III All-American - 4th & 1st
- 3x Academic Scholar All-American
- 2x Middle Atlantic Conference Champion
- Lycoming College Single-Season Leader for Wins (46 in 2001)
- Lycoming College All-Time Wins (127) and Pins (51) Leader
- Lycoming College Graduate Magna Cum Laude Class of 2001
- 3x PIAA High School AA State Qualifier
- 2x PIAA High School AA State Placewinner, (5th & 6th)
- Hughesville High School Class of 1997 Valedictorian
- Inductee into the Lycoming College Athletic Hall of Fame, West Branch Valley Chapter of the Pennsylvania Sports Hall of Fame & Pennsylvania District IV Wrestling Hall of Fame

About The Author

I started wrestling when I was five years old. I have been involved with wrestling for over thirty years now. I wrestled throughout elementary and high school with one goal in mind and that was to be a high school state champion. After falling short on accomplishing that goal, the goals shifted to collegiate wrestling at Lycoming College. The new goal was to be the freshman starter on the wrestling team and it evolved into wanting to be a National Champion. In 2001, my senior year of college, I was finally able to stand on top of the podium and claim the 157 pound Division III Wrestling title. For over 16 years, I had competed and trained in the sport of wrestling to be the best I could be and work towards my goals. Now, 16 years later, it seems like a lifetime ago. I am married with three children of my own and the days of competing on the wrestling mats are a distant memory. The things that once seemed so important to me when I was younger are no longer priorities in my life. Life has changed, but I am thankful and grateful for the experience and the opportunities that were afforded me.

Wrestling has helped shape me into who I am today. There is no doubt that the sport of wrestling has impacted my life greatly. But, as I look back on my career and my life, I also know that as much as wrestling influenced me, my faith in Jesus Christ influenced me more. The more I grow and understand who Christ is and what He did for me, the more I can see His characteristics and influence in my life. In fact, the very same characteristics that I thought were so essential to being a successful wrestler were the ones that Christ himself possessed and taught about in the Bible. I hope that this book helps encourage you in your faith and give you a Biblical perspective on character traits that you may not have thought about before.

What you believe shapes your worldview. Your worldview determines how you see the world and interpret it and therefore act as a result of it. I believe in Jesus Christ. I believe in an afterlife. I believe that we become more than just dirt when we die. I believe our spirit goes to heaven or hell. I believe we were born in God's image with a mind to know God, emotions to love God and a will to choose to obey God. I believe the Bible was written by men and inspired by God and is therefore flawless like God. I believe that our belief and faith in Jesus Christ is the only way to an eternal life with Him. I believe that Christ, God in the form of man, died, was buried and rose on the third day as payment for my sin and that my faith in THAT alone is how I am saved and how I inherit the kingdom of Heaven. I believe that once we believe in Jesus that we are born again and therefore God's children and will not lose our salvation. I believe our purpose is to make much of Him and to be used for His will. That is what I believe. Those beliefs shape who I am and how I view the world. But, what about you? What do you believe? No matter what you believe, I hope that this book challenges and encourages you in your faith and points you to Jesus Christ.

The Purpose

"Wrestling with Jesus" is a 30-day devotional that focuses on building faith and building character. This book is directed primarily to wrestlers, however, it can apply to any athlete and any sport. The purpose of this book is to encourage readers in their faith of Jesus Christ and to look to the Bible and it's teachings to develop and understand character traits of successful athletes and people.

"Wrestling with Jesus" can be understood in either of two ways. In one way, the word wrestling is referring to a struggle. So, think of it as "The Struggle with Jesus". This refers to the struggles you face with your faith and daily walk. The struggle with believing Jesus is who He says He is and did what He said He did. The struggle with accepting Jesus as your own personal Savior that died in your place as payment for your sins. The struggle with walking with Jesus in your daily life. The struggle with understanding and discerning what is truth and what are the lies. The struggle with overcoming your personal sin problems. The struggle with trusting God on a daily basis and living for Him and not yourself. All of these areas are areas that you will struggle with or have struggled in your life. So my hope is that this book will serve as encouragement in your struggles and help you overcome some of your doubts and set backs.

The second meaning of "Wrestling with Jesus" refers to the actual sport of wrestling. That as a wrestler and believer of Jesus Christ, you embody and display the characteristics of Jesus while you participate in the sport. That you embrace all of the characteristics of who He is and what He represents. After reviewing all thirty of the characteristics that most coaches would agree are necessary to become a champion athlete, my hope is that you find those characteristics are the same characteristics that Jesus Christ himself possessed and the Bible teaches about. My hope is that this book may give you a biblical perspective of each of these characteristics and that you pursue after Jesus to attain them so that others may see Him in and through you.

Like wrestling, life can present you with unexpected challenges and opportunities. This devotion is meant to encourage and motivate you in your pursuits on and off the wrestling mat. "Wrestling with Jesus" is about making Jesus the center of your life. By pursuing Jesus, you can fulfill all of the characteristics required to be a successful wrestler and more importantly, a successful man of God. Ultimately, I hope this book encourages you to believe and accept Jesus Christ as your Lord and Savior and live your life to reach others and make much of Him.

Table of Contents

CHARACTER BUILDING

30 DAY DEVOTIONAL

character [kar-ik-ter]
the aggregate of features and traits that
form the individual nature of some person
or thing; moral or ethical quality.

WRES†LING
with Jesus

Talent is a gift, but character is a choice.

John C. Maxwell

Character is the foundation for success and happiness. Just as no worthy building can be erected on a weak foundation, no lasting success or happiness can be built on a weak character.
Michael Josephson

The true test of a man's character is what he does when no one is watching.

John Wooden

Perseverance [pur-suh-veer-uh ns]

steady persistence in a course of action, a purpose, a state, etc., especially in spite of difficulties, obstacles, or discouragement.

Perseverance is one of those characteristics that every great athlete must have in order to be a champion. Why is it so important? In order to have success, it requires much failure in the process. Failure is temporary if we use it to motivate us. Every day that you are training, you not only will fail but you should fail. To improve, you have to push your boundaries and your physical and mental limits. Your body is an incredible creation that has the capacity to do great things and to overcome limits. Push yourself to failure and you will find that the next day you can do one more rep, or take one more step, or go just a little harder. You must fail in order to succeed. The test of a true champion is their ability to overcome obstacles and failures and to endure and maintain their course of action in order to obtain the goal. All great athletes have struggled in their pursuit of greatness and all great athletes have failed. Failure breeds success if we persevere through the trials. The key is to never quit and to get back up and continue on when we fall down or fall short. That is the only way to truly succeed.

If we look at the Bible you can see perseverance as a pillar to who Jesus Christ is and who His followers were. Jesus himself suffered and showed tremendous perseverance to finish the mission He was sent to earth to complete. He was beaten to near death, forced to carry a heavy cross miles up a hill and then hung on that cross to die for you and me as an atoning sacrifice for our sins. His follower, Paul, endured great suffering and exemplified the characteristic of perseverance in order to spread the gospel throughout the world. Paul was stoned and left for dead, beaten and whipped, shipwrecked, criticized for his faith by his peers, bitten by a viper, jailed and run out of multiple towns and yet, he marched on towards his mission of spreading the gospel. He did not let these major obstacles and trials deter him from his mission. Both Jesus and Paul displayed tremendous perseverance in order to achieve their goals.

The reality is that in life, we will face trials. We will face hardships and we will face loss. Whether it is on the wrestling mat, in the practice room or in life in general, it is not a matter of if we face trials but when and how often. The question will be "how will you respond"? You can allow those losses and your sufferings to drag you down and eventually force you to quit trying and give up. That is one option. The other option is that you can persevere and push through it and continue on your path to victory. To finish the race that you started and continue to pursue your goals. The choice is yours, but the good news is that you do not have to do it alone. You can rely on Jesus and He can endure it with you. In Matthew 11:28, Jesus says, "come to me, all you who are weary and burdened, and I will give you rest." It is in our weakness, that the Lord's strength and power is made evident. Seek him during your trials and continue to run the race all the way to the finish line. In Philippians 4:13, Paul says, "I can do all things through Him who strengthens me." Whether you are winning or whether you are losing on the wrestling mat or in life, this also holds true for you. Make Jesus the center of your life and you will find His strength to persevere through any trials you face here on earth.

Reflection: Is there an area of my life that I am failing to persevere through? Am I trying to do it with my own strength or am I seeking God for His guidance and help?

Prayer: Lord, I need You. My burdens are too much for me to bare. I trust You with my life. You are in control. Help me to persevere through these tough times. Help me keep my faith. Thank You, Lord, for the many blessings that I have in my life. Let me always have a thankful heart. Amen.

Perseverance

"I've missed more than 9000 shots in my career. I've lost almost 300 games. 26 times I've been trusted to take the game winning shot and missed. I've failed over and over and over again in my life. And that is why I succeed."

- Michael Jordan

Perseverance [pur-suh-veer-uh ns]

*steady persistence in a course of action, a purpose, a state, etc., especially in spite of difficulties, obstacles, or discouragem*ent.

Romans 5:3-5
Not only so, but we also glory in our sufferings, because we know that suffering produces perseverance; perseverance, character; and character, hope. And hope does not put us to shame, because God's love has been poured out into our hearts through the Holy Spirit, who has been given to us.

Hebrews 12:1
Therefore, since we are surrounded by such a great cloud of witnesses, let us throw off everything that hinders and the sin that so easily entangles. And let us run with perseverance the race marked out for us, fixing our eyes on Jesus, the pioneer and perfecter of faith.

James 1:12
Blessed is the one who perseveres under trial because, having stood the test, that person will receive the crown of life that the Lord has promised to those who love him.

Galatians 6:9
Let us not become weary in doing good, for at the proper time we will reap a harvest if we do not give up.

1 Corinthians 15:58
Therefore, my dear brothers and sisters, stand firm. Let nothing move you. Always give yourselves fully to the work of the Lord, because you know that your labor in the Lord is not in vain.

James 1:2-4
Consider it pure joy, my brothers and sisters, whenever you face trials of many kinds, because you know that the testing of your faith produces perseverance. Let perseverance finish its work so that you may be mature and complete, not lacking anything.

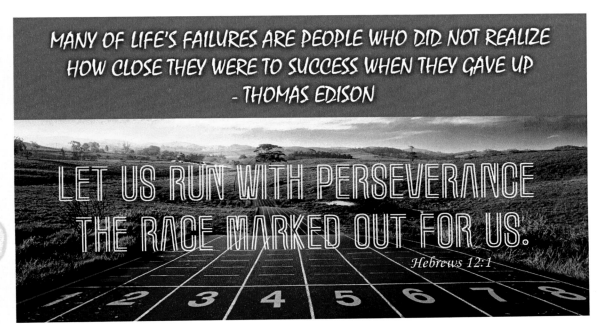

MANY OF LIFE'S FAILURES ARE PEOPLE WHO DID NOT REALIZE HOW CLOSE THEY WERE TO SUCCESS WHEN THEY GAVE UP
- THOMAS EDISON

LET US RUN WITH PERSEVERANCE THE RACE MARKED OUT FOR US.
Hebrews 12:1

Courage [kur-ij]

the quality of mind or spirit that enables a person to face difficulty, danger, pain without fear; bravery.

They say courage is the ability to act without fear. I disagree with that definition of courage. I believe courage is the willingness to act in spite of fear. We may be afraid or fearful, but courage is about going forward anyway. Theodore Roosevelt once said, "Courage is not having the strength to go on; it is going on when you don't have the strength." It takes courage to walk out on a wrestling mat and face an opponent. There is no one out there that can help you but you. It is just you and your opponent in front of a crowded gym and everyone is watching you. Anxiety and fear can easily consume you and make you feel paralyzed in that situation, but yet time after time, you go out on that mat anyway to do battle. The great thing about the sport of wrestling is that on any given day, no matter if you have lost to that opponent before or what they are ranked, you can still win and it all is determined by you. You cannot blame your teammates, you cannot blame your coaches, you cannot blame anyone but you because you are the one in the arena and you are the one that is doing battle. It takes courage to pursue a sport that demands so much. It takes courage to face another man that may be stronger, or faster or more skilled than you. It takes courage to just show up and put yourself at risk of failure.

When we are faced with times or situations that cause us fear, we can look to Jesus and the Bible for encouragement. When Jesus was in the Garden of Gethsemane, He prayed that God the Father would take this cup from Him if it was His will. Jesus was referring to the suffering and death that He was about to endure on the cross. Jesus knew what was coming and He was fearful. Jesus was in such anguish the scripture says "that His sweat was like drops of blood falling to the ground". Despite all of this agony over what He knew was coming, Jesus trusted in the Lord that His plans were best and He continued forward to achieve the mission He was called to do by God the Father. Jesus displayed great courage in the face of monumental trials because He knew that God was in control.

Another instance of great courage in the Bible is the story of David and Goliath. Three thousand years ago, in the Valley of Elah, a massive man named Goliath stepped out of the Philistine ranks to defy and taunt the army of Israel and their God. For forty days, he taunted the Israelite warriors, shaming them and daring any of them to a fight to the death and challenging them to a winner take all battle. Every morning, the Israelites failed to answer the challenge until a teenage Hebrew shepherd boy named David showed up in the camp. After hearing the giant pour out his scorn, David, who was outmatched, undersized and clearly the underdog volunteered to face Goliath. The result was shocking. David took his shepherd's sling, grabbed a few small stones and went out to battle the giant. David knocked out Goliath by striking him in the head with a small stone and then chopped off his head. As a result, David saved Israel from the Philistines. Where did David's courage come from? Did he just muster it up from within himself? The answer is no. Just like Jesus in the Garden, David's strength and courage came from his faith and trust in the Lord. David was not self-confident, he was God-confident. We will all face "giants" in our lives whether it is in a battle on the wrestling mat or it is in the trials of life. Our confidence and courage comes from our faith in the Lord that He is in control and that He is with us always. We must always have the courage to do what is right and know that it is His strength in us and through Him that will help us move forward in times of fear. Be courageous!

Reflection: Is there an area of my life I need to be courageous and face my fears?

Prayer: Lord, I know my courage comes from You and through You. Give me the strength today to face my fears and to push forward. Thank You, Lord. Amen.

Courage [kur-ij]

the quality of mind or spirit that enables a person to face difficulty, danger, pain without fear; bravery.

Deuteronomy 31:6
Be strong and courageous. Do not be afraid or terrified because of them, for the Lord your God goes with you; he will never leave you nor forsake you.

1 Chronicles 28:20
David also said to Solomon his son, "Be strong and courageous, and do the work. Do not be afraid or discouraged, for the LORD God, my God, is with you. He will not fail you or forsake you until all the work for the service of the temple of the LORD is finished."

Psalm 31:24
Be strong and take heart, all you who hope in the LORD

Isaiah 41:10-13
So do not fear, for I am with you; do not be dismayed, for I am your God. I will strengthen you and help you; I will uphold you with my righteous right hand. "All who rage against you will surely be ashamed and disgraced; those who oppose you will be as nothing and perish. Though you search for your enemies, you will not find them. Those who wage war against you will be as nothing at all. For I am the LORD your God who takes hold of your right hand and says to you, Do not fear; I will help you.

Psalm 23:4
Even though I walk through the darkest valley, I will fear no evil, for you are with me; your rod and your staff, they comfort me.

Psalm 27:1
The LORD is my light and my salvation—whom shall I fear? The LORD is the stronghold of my life—of whom shall I be afraid?

2 Timothy 1:7
For the Spirit God gave us does not make us timid, but gives us power, love and self-discipline.

Joshua 1:9
Have I not commanded you? Be strong and courageous. Do not be afraid; do not be discouraged, for the LORD your God will be with you wherever you go."

1 Corinthians 15:58
Therefore, my dear brothers and sisters, stand firm. Let nothing move you. Always give yourselves fully to the work of the Lord, because you know that your labor in the Lord is not in vain.

1 Corinthians 16:3
Be on your guard; stand firm in the faith; be courageous; be strong.

Ephesians 6:10
Finally, be strong in the Lord and in his mighty power.

Psalm 56:3-4
When I am afraid, I put my trust in you. In God, whose word I praise—in God I trust and am not afraid. What can mere mortals do to me?

i learned that
COURAGE
WAS NOT THE
ABSENCE OF FEAR,
BUT THE
TRIUMPH
OVER IT.
THE BRAVE MAN
IS NOT HE WHO DOES NOT
FEEL AFRAID,
BUT HE WHO
CONQUERS THAT FEAR
-NELSON MANDELA-

Humble [huhm-buh l]

not proud or arrogant; modest:

Being humble and showing humility is not a weakness. There is a big difference between confidence and being conceited and arrogant. Being humble is a desirable characteristic that every wrestler should have. Being humble recognizes that it is not all about you. It recognizes that there can always be improvement and that there is always someone better. Every great wrestler has lost. Being boastful of your accomplishment is self-focused and prideful. Being humble recognizes that there were coaches, family, teammates and others along the way that have helped you achieve your success. Being humble is about respecting the sport, your opponents and those that came before you. It is about being thankful for the talents that you have and the opportunity to compete. C.S. Lewis wrote, "True humility is not thinking less of yourself. It's thinking of yourself less." This comes back to the goal of being others focused. How can you help your teammates? How can you help the guy next to you be successful as well? These are qualities that endure and that leave a lasting impression rather than self-aggrandizing your own accomplishments. Be humbly confident!

Success in any sport can cause you to become self-focused and think that you are better than everyone else. This thought process tends to bring out the worst in your character. It is the opposite of what God desires for you. Fortunately, wrestling has the ability to humble you very quickly because there is always someone better than you on any given day. Be confident in your abilities, but be humble as well.

If anyone in the history of the world had a reason to be boastful and proud it would be Jesus. This is a man that was in fact God in the flesh. He was able to do amazing and supernatural feats like calming the sea, walking on water, turning water into wine, healing the blind, the sick and the lepers. He could make the paralyzed walk and even raise people from the dead. There was no one in the world that was more powerful yet, He was the most humble of men that ever lived. Jesus came to serve. This was the King of the World and yet, He considered himself a servant. He came not for himself, but for others. To be used by God and for God. That is a humbling thought and that is what you are to do as well. Your purpose is to not make much of yourself, but to make much of Him. You are to be others focused, not self-focused.

The greatest man in history, had no servants, yet they called him Master. He had no degree, yet they called him Teacher. He had no medicines, yet they called him Healer. He had no army, yet kings feared Him. He won no military battles, yet He conquered the world. He committed no crime, yet they crucified Him. He was buried in a tomb, yet He lives today. His name is Jesus. Be thankful, be humble and use your gifts and your talents to build others up and help make those around you better.

Reflection: Am I being boastful and proud? Or am I considering others first rather than myself? Am I reflecting Jesus's servanthood in my life? Am I striving for my own glory or to make much of Jesus through my opportunities?

Prayer: Lord, I have areas of my life that have caused me to be boastful and proud. Help me to consider others better than myself so that I become more others focused than self-focused. Thank You for the talents that You have given me. I pray that You show me how I can use them to reach others for You. Amen.

WORK FOR A CAUSE, NOT FOR APPLAUSE. LIVE LIFE TO EXPRESS, NOT TO IMPRESS. DON'T STRIVE TO MAKE YOUR PRESENCE NOTICED, JUST MAKE YOUR ABSENCE FELT

- UNKNOWN

Humble [huhm-buh l]

not proud or arrogant; modest:

Ephesians 4:2
Be completely humble and gentle; be patient, bearing with one another in love.

Philippians 2:3
Do nothing out of selfish ambition or vain conceit. Rather, in humility value others above yourselves.

Proverbs 11:2
When pride comes, then comes disgrace, but with humility comes wisdom.

James 4:10
Humble yourselves before the Lord, and he will lift you up.

Provers 2:4
Humility is the fear of the Lord; its wages are riches and honor and life.

1 Peter 5:6
Humble yourselves, therefore, under God's mighty hand, that he may lift you up in due time

Matthew 11:29-30
Take my yoke upon you and learn from me, for I am gentle and humble in heart, and you will find rest for your souls. For my yoke is easy and my burden is light.

Proverbs 18:22
Before a downfall the heart is haughty, but humility comes before honor.

1 Peter 3:8
Finally, all of you, be like-minded, be sympathetic, love one another, be compassionate and humble.

Mark 9:35
Sitting down, Jesus called the Twelve and said, "Anyone who wants to be first must be the very last, and the servant of all."

Philippians 4:20
To our God and Father be glory for ever and ever. Amen.

Matthew 23:12
For those who exalt themselves will be humbled, and those who humble themselves will be exalted.

> Humility is not thinking less of yourself but thinking of yourself less.
> -C.S. Lewis

Leadership [lee-der-ship]

the position or function of a leader, a person who guides or directs a group.

They say actions speak louder than words. I agree with that statement, especially when it comes to leadership. It is a hard task to lead from behind. If you are not pushing hard and giving your best effort, then how can you expect your teammates to give their best efforts? The best leaders lead by example. They are the ones that put the extra time in, do the extra rep, go the extra mile, push their teammates by building them up and encouraging them to be better. These type of leaders inspire and motivate. They are leading by example and their attitude becomes contagious to the rest of the room. Good leadership takes strength of character and a firm commitment. This means doing what you say, when you say it. A great leader is someone that is willing to do the work that they expect from everyone else. Leading by example will earn you respect, credibility and loyalty among your teammates. It will create a culture of improvement and a desire to strive for excellence.

In order to be a great leader you should first make your words count. Then those words should inspire action. And finally, your actions should back up your words. If you are saying one thing and doing another, then it will be very difficult to inspire anyone. Your actions and the effort you are displaying is being witnessed by your teammates. Have you ever heard the saying "if you talk the talk, then you better be able to walk the walk"? It means if you say something, then you have to follow through with it. Larry Bird said, "Leadership is getting players to believe in you. If you tell a teammate you're ready to play as tough as you're able to, you'd better go out there and do it. Players will see right through a phony. And they can tell when you're not giving it all you've got." Lead by example by giving your best effort.

Perhaps, the greatest and most influential leaders of all time was Jesus Christ. Jesus had told his Disciples that they would suffer for His name. He not only told them that they would suffer but that they should expect it. He said that they should expect to be persecuted if they chose to follow Him. In fact, Jesus paints a pretty gloomy picture of what His followers were going to endure if they followed Him. He said that many of them would likely be beaten, shamed, scorned, imprisoned or even be killed for their faith if they followed Him. Yet, His disciples followed him anyway. Why? Why would anyone follow someone that would lead them to their own demise? Because Jesus stood for something that His followers could believe in. Jesus's words were not just words, they were action. Jesus's followers witnessed His words in action over and over again. They believed in Him and believed in the purpose and cause of what He was saying. His words and His example inspired action. His followers would have followed Him anywhere even if it meant to their own deaths. And for many of His followers, it did lead to their deaths. However, over 2000 years later, because those first believers were willing to follow Jesus's leadership, we are still hearing and preaching the gospel today. And yes, today, Jesus's followers are still being persecuted all over the world for their faith. And yet, they continue to follow Him. Followers of Christ still believe and trust Jesus's leading. That is a testament of great leadership. So get out there and lead by example by believing in what you say and backing it up with your actions.

Reflection: Are my words just words? Or do my actions match my words? Am I leading by example? Am I being a good leader to my teammates? Am I putting in the effort that I need to?

Prayer: Lord, help me to back up my words with my actions. Help me to be a good leader to my teammates. Show me discernment on how I can improve as a leader. Thank You, Lord, for the opportunity to guide others to achieve their goals. Amen.

Leadership [lee-der-ship]

the position or function of a leader, a person who guides or directs a group.

Luke 6:31
Do to others as you would have them do to you.

Philippaisn 3:17
Join together in following my example, brothers and sisters, and just as you have us as a model, keep your eyes on those who live as we do

1 Peter 5:3
not lording it over those entrusted to you, but being examples to the flock.

Philippians 2:3
Do nothing out of selfish ambition or vain conceit. Rather, in humility value others above yourselves,

John 10:11
I am the good shepherd. The good shepherd lays down his life for the sheep.

Hebrews 13:7
Remember your leaders, who spoke the word of God to you. Consider the outcome of their way of life and imitate their faith.

1 Thessalonians 5:12
Now we ask you, brothers and sisters, to acknowledge those who work hard among you, who care for you in the Lord and who admonish you.

Matthew 20:28
just as the Son of Man did not come to be served, but to serve, and to give his life as a ransom for many.

1 Timothy 4:12
Don't let anyone look down on you because you are young, but set an example for the believers in speech, in conduct, in love, in faith and in purity.

Titus 1:7
Since an overseer manages God's household, he must be blameless—not overbearing, not quick-tempered, not given to drunkenness, not violent, not pursuing dishonest gain.

1 Corinthians 11:1
Follow my example, as I follow the example of Christ

1 Peter 5:2
Be shepherds of God's flock that is under your care, watching over them—not because you must, but because you are willing, as God wants you to be; not pursuing dishonest gain, but eager to serve

Titus 2:7-8
In everything set them an example by doing what is good. In your teaching show integrity, seriousness and soundness of speech that cannot be condemned, so that those who oppose you may be ashamed because they have nothing bad to say about us.

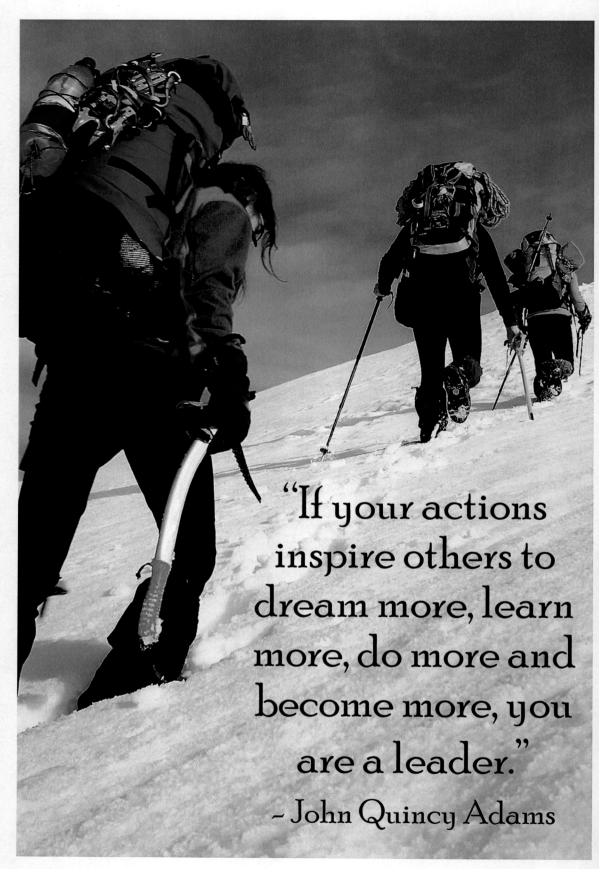

"If your actions inspire others to dream more, learn more, do more and become more, you are a leader."

– John Quincy Adams

Positivity [poz-i-tiv-i-tee]

The state or character of being positive. a good, affirmative, or constructive quality or attribute

Your mind is the most powerful part of your body and it is usually the most neglected aspect of training for an athlete. One of the most overused clichés is that your performance is 90% mental. But the truth is, it is 100% accurate. The problem is that 90% of coaches and athletes spend all of their time working on the physical and fundamental aspects of the sport. While that is extremely important, the mind and your mindset is probably the most important key to success when it comes to wrestling. Your mind is what separates the good wrestlers from the great wrestlers. The great wrestlers learn to push through barriers, to find the next gear, to overcome adversity, to keep going when they don't have anymore in the tank, to stay calm in the midst of a storm, to have the discipline to get their sleep or eat properly, to say "no thanks" when everyone else is doing it. Those actions all come from your mind and having the proper mindset. These qualities don't happen by accident, it takes training.

Your thoughts influence your actions and then your actions influence your thoughts. How do you approach a match? How do you respond when things don't go your way? What happens when you get tired? What happens if you are losing? Your mind controls your body and when your mind isn't right, your body doesn't respond the way you want it to. You panic, you freeze up, and then you fold. What you put into your mind usually also comes out of it. Henry Ford once said, "If you think you can, or you think you can't—you're right." What he is saying is that if you believe you are going to lose the match before you ever walk out on the mat, then chances are you probably will. Negativity leads to doubt, doubt leads to fear and fear can be paralyzing. I have seen the most physically gifted wrestlers with better technique and a better skill set than their opponents completely fall apart on the wrestling mat because of mental breakdowns. Negative thinking will destroy you on a wrestling mat. Positive thinking leads to confidence and belief in your abilities to persevere and continue moving forward. Positivity creates perseverance and perseverance creates hope. You are never out of a match until the last whistle blows. You can't lose if you never give up, no matter what the score says at the end.

Maybe this is why Jesus talks so much about renewing your mind. He knows that your mind controls your actions and you have to hold captive every thought. Jesus had a very positive message in His teachings. He teaches to not to be afraid, to not worry about anything, to not judge others, to forgive others including your enemies and to rejoice always and in everything give thanks. His follower Paul continued to preach a positive message. In Philippians 4:8, he talks directly about what you should set your mind on. You are to think on things that are true, that are noble, things that are right and pure, things that are lovely and admirable, and things that are excellent and praiseworthy. What you feed into your minds typically comes out in your actions.

There is a story I heard that really impacted me. It says there is a black dog and a white dog inside of you doing battle. The black dog possesses qualities typically associated as negative, including envy, greed, sorrow, anger, resentment, and arrogance. The white dog possesses qualities understood as positive, including love, joy, kindness, empathy, compassion, humility, and peace. The question is asked, in the battle, "which dog will win the fight?" The answer is, "Whichever one you feed." The Bible clearly leads you in a direction of positive thinking in your walk with God. As a believer, you have the power of God to discipline your thinking and control your thoughts. The choice is always yours.

Reflection: Am I allowing my circumstances to dictate my attitude? Am I filling my thoughts with negativity or am I choosing to rise above my trials and renew my mind?

Prayer: Lord, thank You for the many blessings in my life. Thank You for renewing each day. Please help me to have a positive mindset despite my circumstances. Amen.

KEEP YOUR THOUGHTS POSITIVE
BECAUSE YOUR THOUGHTS BECOME

YOUR WORDS

KEEP YOUR WORDS POSITIVE
BECAUSE YOUR WORDS BECOME

YOUR BEHAVIOR

KEEP YOUR BEHAVIOR POSITIVE
BECAUSE YOUR BEHAVIOR BECOMES

YOUR HABITS

KEEP YOUR HABITS POSITIVE
BECAUSE YOUR HABITS BECOME

YOUR VALUES

KEEP YOUR VALUES POSITIVE
BECAUSE YOUR VALUES BECOME

YOUR DESTINY

MAHATMA GANDHI

Positivity [poz-i-tiv-i-tee]

The state or character of being positive. a good, affirmative, or constructive quality or attribute

Philippians 4:6-13
Do not be anxious about anything, but in every situation, by prayer and petition, with thanksgiving, present your requests to God. And the peace of God, which transcends all understanding, will guard your hearts and your minds in Christ Jesus.

Finally, brothers and sisters, whatever is true, whatever is noble, whatever is right, whatever is pure, whatever is lovely, whatever is admirable—if anything is excellent or praiseworthy—think about such things. Whatever you have learned or received or heard from me, or seen in me—put it into practice. And the God of peace will be with you.

Proverbs 17:22
A cheerful heart is good medicine, but a crushed spirit dries up the bones.

Ephesians 5:20
always giving thanks to God the Father for everything, in the name of our Lord Jesus Christ.

Colossians 4:2
Devote yourselves to prayer, being watchful and thankful.

Proverbs 3:5
Trust in the Lord with all your heart and lean not on your own understanding

Romans 12:2
Do not conform to the pattern of this world, but be transformed by the renewing of your mind. Then you will be able to test and approve what God's will is—his good, pleasing and perfect will.

Hebrews 13:6
So we say with confidence, "The Lord is my helper; I will not be afraid.
What can mere mortals do to me?"

1 Corinthians 10:31
So whether you eat or drink or whatever you do, do it all for the glory of God.

Colossians 3:2
Set your minds on things above, not on earthly things.

WHAT CONSUMES YOUR MIND, CONTROLS YOUR LIFE.

"When we fill our thoughts with RIGHT things, the WRONG ones have no room to enter"

-Joyce Meyer

Hard Worker [hahrd] [wur-ker]

A laborer that displays great exertion and vigor; works strenuously.

There is no substitute for hard work. If you want to achieve your goals the only way to do it is by putting in the time and embracing the grind. You can't just hope for success. In order to achieve success, you need the strength of mind and body to struggle and work hard to train and reach your full potential. Hard work is not fun. Work is a laborious exertion directed to produce or accomplish something. There is no substitute for hard work, if you want to obtain your goals. This attribute separates the good from the great. Most times if two wrestlers of equal strength, equal talent and equal skill set face off, the winner will likely be the one who trained the hardest. Vince Lombardi once said, "The man on top of the mountain didn't fall there." You need to remember that there are no short cuts to the top. It is straight up and it is going to hurt. It is going to take everything you have in order to plant that flag at the top of the mountain. You are going to have to dig deep within yourself to see what you are made of. When you are completely exhausted and you don't have anything left in the tank, keep going. That is the path to success and achieving your goals. That is embracing the grind.

In order to seize the opportunities in front of you, you have to be able to control the things that you can control and work hard to improve in those areas. You can control your diet, you can control your rest, you can control how hard you are training, and you can control your attitude and mental preparation. You can control everything leading up to your match. If you take care of and continue to work to improve the little things, then the big things will take care of themselves. When you control the controllables like your attitude, your effort and your preparation then the results will take care of themselves.

When I was a collegiate wrestler, I asked myself daily, "Am I working harder than everyone else?" If I believed I was working harder than everyone else, then I developed a confidence and a belief in myself that I deserved it more than my opponents. That created a motivation and determination to refuse to lose to anyone. I believed that I deserved it more because I believed that I worked harder than my opponents and that my opponents were trying to take that away from me. All of the sacrifice, all of the pain, all of reps, all of the time that I had dedicated to reach my goals was being challenged and threatened. It caused me to be more determined and more resolved to win. Your mind is a powerful tool. When you combine belief and hard work together it can become an unstoppable force. Had I not put in all of that hard work, then I may not have found the motivation or sense of purpose to rise to the challenges each time I walked on that mat.

The Bible references the idea of hard work quite extensively. Work is to be a major part of your life. It contrasts working hard versus laziness and teaches that diligence pays off. It refers to reaping what you sow. you are to work hard while serving the Lord. It demonstrates with hard work you can accomplish many things. It refers to how your hard work can influence others in a positive way. God has a lot to say in the Bible about work, your attitude toward it and the results of it in your life. These are timeless principles that apply in any age. Hard work pays in the end—in so many ways! Working hard and doing your best is what Christ expects of you as His child. You are to be an example for others at work by keeping a strong sense of faith and spirit to guide your actions. Colossians 3:23 says, "Whatever you do, work heartily, as for the Lord and not for men.

Reflection: Am I working hard? Am I giving my best effort? Are there areas of my life that I could improve on? Am I willing to put in the necessary work?

Prayer: Lord, thank You for my ability to work. I pray that You give me the strength to work hard today and that the work that I do and the way I do it brings hope, life and encouragement to those I come in contact with today. Amen.

SUCCESS

Is

the SUM of

SMALL

efforts,

Repeated

DAY IN AND DAY OUT

(R COLLIER)

THE PRICE OF SUCCESS IS
HARD WORK, DEDICATION TO
THE JOB AT HAND, AND THE
DETERMINATION THAT
WHETHER WE WIN OR LOSE, WE
HAVE APPLIED THE BEST OF
OURSELVES TO THE
TASK AT HAND.
-VINCE LOMBARDI

THE ONLY PLACE SUCCESS COMES BEFORE WORK IS IN THE DICTIONARY.

-VINCE LOMBARDI

Hard Worker [hahrd] [wur-ker]

A laborer that displays great exertion and vigor; works strenuously.

Colossians 3:17
And whatever you do, whether in word or deed, do it all in the name of the Lord Jesus, giving thanks to God the Father through him.

Ephesians 2:10
For we are God's handiwork, created in Christ Jesus to do good works, which God prepared in advance for us to do.

1 Corinthians 9:27
No, I strike a blow to my body and make it my slave so that after I have preached to others, I myself will not be disqualified for the prize.

Matthew 5:16
In the same way, let your light shine before others, that they may see your good deeds and glorify your Father in heaven.

Romans 12:11-12
Never be lacking in zeal, but keep your spiritual fervor, serving the Lord. Be joyful in hope, patient in affliction, faithful in prayer.

Psalm 90:17
May the favor of the Lord our God rest on us; establish the work of our hands for us—yes, establish the work of our hands.

Proverbs 18:9
One who is slack in his work is brother to one who destroys

Colossians 3:23-24
Whatever you do, work at it with all your heart, as working for the Lord, not for human masters, since you know that you will receive an inheritance from the Lord as a reward. It is the Lord Christ you are serving.

Proverbs 10:4
Lazy hands make for poverty, but diligent hands bring wealth.

Genesis 2:15
The Lord God took the man and put him in the Garden of Eden to work it and take care of it.

Proverbs 16:3
Commit to the Lord whatever you do, and he will establish your plans.

Galatians 6:7
Do not be deceived: God cannot be mocked. A man reaps what he sows.

Colossains 3:23
Whatever you do, work at it with all your heart, as working for the Lord, not for human masters,

John 5:17
In his defense Jesus said to them, "My Father is always at his work to this very day, and I too am working."

Teamwork [teem-wurk]

cooperative or coordinated effort on the part of a group of persons acting together as a team or in the interests of a common cause.

They say that wrestling is an individual sport. While that may be true for the six or seven minutes that you are out on the wrestling mat, the reality is that your team plays a vital role in your individual success. Besides the practical application of needing a partner to drill with, your teammates have a significant influence in your performance. Many times the team comradery dictates the attitude of the entire team. Your attitude affects your training and your training affects your performance. If the team as a whole is working for a common goal and each teammate is on the same page of the vision, then the performance of the team is elevated. I cannot emphasize enough how important good teammates are to your success. Through teamwork, you can receive encouragement, be challenged and pushed to your limits, receive solid instruction and advice, be picked up when you are down, and build friendships that will last a lifetime.

I can say with 100% certainty that I would not have reached my individual goals without the teammates and coaches that I have had in my life. I was blessed to have individuals on my wrestling teams that were like-minded and driven to achieve the same results as I wanted. It did not matter if the guys I practiced with each day were starters on the team or practice room wrestlers, they all played a vital role in my growth and improvements each day. I respected them because they were making me better. Teamwork helps with training, development and support which are all critical in your growth on and off the mat. I can remember countless nights of working out together with some of my teammates in the weight room, or running, or drilling technique, or going live in the mat room, or riding the bike to get that extra pound off. There was always someone next to me enduring it with me. Without their support and push, it would have been very difficult to motivate myself and to keep moving forward. To pick myself up and go one more round. My teammates exemplified teamwork and for that I am thankful and blessed.

While the word teamwork does not appear in the Bible, the Word of God does contain a lot of information about working together which is what teamwork is all about. You are designed to need God and each other. The truth is no one has all the skills, gifts, or wisdom. It is learned and passed down from those that came before you or those that are working beside you. God has blessed you with various gifts and talents. These gifts and talents are not meant to be kept to yourself but to be used to serve one another. God has blessed you and you are to use that blessing for the good of those around you. Proverbs 27:17 says, "Iron sharpens iron, and one man sharpens another".

Jesus recognized the importance of a team because He assembled a 12 man team Himself, the disciples. That team was marked by diversity. Although the individuals came from quite different backgrounds, careers and skill-sets, they worked together for one common purpose which was to spread the Gospel of Jesus Christ. A biblical model of teamwork puts God as the established leader in every team to create strength in unity. If you can put your individual wants aside and think of how to improve the lives of those around you on your team, the reality is that you will grow more in the process as the whole team improves. So, be a good teammate!

Reflection: Am I being a good teammate? Am I working together with my teammates for a common goal? What can I do to help my teammates improve?

Prayer: Lord, I am thankful for my teammates, my coaches and my family for their support. Help me to see and fulfill the needs of those around me so that we can all improve and achieve more. Thank You for the blessing of my team. Amen.

Teamwork [teem-wurk]

cooperative or coordinated effort on the part of a group of persons acting together as a team or in the interests of a common cause.

Ecclesiastes 4:9–12
Two are better than one, because they have a good return for their labor: If either of them falls down,one can help the other up. But pity anyone who falls and has no one to help them up. Also, if two lie down together, they will keep warm. But how can one keep warm alone? Though one may be overpowered, two can defend themselves. A cord of three strands is not quickly broken.

Proverbs 27:17
As iron sharpens iron, so one person sharpens another.

1 Corinthians 12:20-26
As it is, there are many parts, but one body. The eye cannot say to the hand, "I don't need you!" And the head cannot say to the feet, "I don't need you!" On the contrary, those parts of the body that seem to be weaker are indispensable, and the parts that we think are less honorable we treat with special honor. And the parts that are unpresentable are treated with special modesty, while our presentable parts need no special treatment. But God has put the body together, giving greater honor to the parts that lacked it, so that there should be no division in the body, but that its parts should have equal concern for each other. If one part suffers, every part suffers with it; if one part is honored, every part rejoices with it.

Philippians 2:1-4
Therefore if you have any encouragement from being united with Christ, if any comfort from his love, if any common sharing in the Spirit, if any tenderness and compassion, then make my joy complete by being like-minded, having the same love, being one in spirit and of one mind. Do nothing out of selfish ambition or vain conceit. Rather, in humility value others above yourselves, not looking to your own interests but each of you to the interests of the others.

Ephesians 4:16
From him the whole body, joined and held together by every supporting ligament, grows and builds itself up in love, as each part does its work.

1 Peter 4:10
Each of you should use whatever gift you have received to serve others, as faithful stewards of God's grace in its various forms.

Romans 15:1
We who are strong ought to bear with the failings of the weak and not to please ourselves.

Galatians 6:2
Carry each other's burdens, and in this way you will fulfill the law of Christ.

Proverbs 11:14
For lack of guidance a nation falls, but victory is won through many advisers.

1 Corinthians 1:10
I appeal to you, brothers and sisters, in the name of our Lord Jesus Christ, that all of you agree with one another in what you say and that there be no divisions among you, but that you be perfectly united in mind and thought.

COMING TOGETHER IS A BEGINNING; KEEPING TOGETHER IS PROGRESS; WORKING TOGETHER IS SUCCESS

-HENRY FORD

Teamwork is the ability to work together toward a common vision. The ability to direct individual accomplishment toward organizational objectives. It is the fuel that allows common people to attain uncommon results.

- Andrew Carnegie

Teachable [tee-chuh-buh l]

capable of being instructed or taught

How can you improve if you are unwilling to learn? Being teachable is an important characteristic for growth. I have been fortunate to be on both sides of the wrestling mat as a student-athlete and as a coach. As a wrestler, I did not fully understand the role of a coach until I became a coach. There is nothing more frustrating as a coach than having a student-athlete that is unwilling to be coached or teachable. Coaches are teachers and their sole purpose is to help you improve your skills and help develop you to your full potential. Sometimes that requires your coach to tell you things that you do not want to hear or to make you do things that you do not want to do or understand why you need to do them.

There are several areas that you can look to improve on to be more teachable. Teachable people have an attitude conducive to learning. They are approachable, attentive and receptive to gaining knowledge. I have been around the sport of wrestling for over 30 years and I am still learning. You can always learn more and you will never know everything. Be a sponge when it comes to gaining knowledge. Approach learning with an open-mindset and realize that everyone has something they can teach you and that every day you can learn something. Have confidence and know that whatever you learn, that knowledge will benefit you in some way.

Teachable people are also able to do self-evaluation. You have to be able to look at your own weaknesses to figure out where you need to improve. You cannot just turn a blind eye to areas that you are failing in and expect them to get better on their own. You have to purposely evaluate and work on those areas of weakness.

Teachable people are able to invite constructive criticism from others into their lives. You need to be able to seek out and accept advice from others. Sometimes you don't realize where you are falling short. Have the courage and the openness to invite others to speak into your life to shed light on areas that you may not see or realize you are lacking in.

Lastly, teachable people are willing to change. You have to be willing to not only listen but to take action in order to improve. You have to be willing to trust your coaches and do the things that you may not want to do. It means stepping out of your comfort zone and accepting change. Change is necessary for improvement.

The scriptures are full of advice about being teachable. There are many references to listening, obeying and heeding God's wisdom: being slow to speak and quick to listen, recognize discipline which may be necessary for instruction and training, respect the wisdom of your elders, and much more. Jesus himself was a teacher and His sole purpose was for you to listen to His words, trust Him and follow Him. That requires you to humble yourself and realize that you have areas of weakness that needs attention. You have to be willing to obey and change if you are to fix the things that are broken in you. The instruction is clear, but the question remains, "Are you going to be teachable?"

Reflection: Am I being teachable? Would a coach want to work with me? What areas of weakness do I need to work on? Am I willing to trust others advice and make a change?

Prayer: Lord, help me to be approachable and willing to learn. Help me to recognize my weaknesses and accept constructive criticism. Lord, give me the strength to be willing to change and to be teachable. Amen.

Teachable [tee-chuh-buh l]

capable of being instructed or taught

1 Peter 5:5
In the same way, you who are younger, submit yourselves to your elders. All of you, clothe yourselves with humility toward one another, because, "God opposes the proud but shows favor to the humble."

Proverbs 13:18
Whoever disregards discipline comes to poverty and shame, but whoever heeds correction is honored.

Proverbs 12:1
Whoever loves discipline loves knowledge, but whoever hates correction is stupid.

2 Timothy 3:16
All Scripture is God-breathed and is useful for teaching, rebuking, correcting and training in righteousness,

Hebrews 12:6
because the Lord disciplines the one he loves, and he chastens everyone he accepts as his son."

Acts 8:31
"How can I," he said, "unless someone explains it to me?" So he invited Philip to come up and sit with him.

Proverbs 22:6
Start children off on the way they should go, and even when they are old they will not turn from it.

2 Peter 3:18
But grow in the grace and knowledge of our Lord and Savior Jesus Christ. To him be glory both now and forever! Amen.

James 1:19
My dear brothers and sisters, take note of this: Everyone should be quick to listen, slow to speak and slow to become angry,

Psalms 27:11
Teach me your way, Lord; lead me in a straight path because of my oppressors.

Proverbs 15:2
The tongue of the wise adorns knowledge, but the mouth of the fool gushes folly.

Psalms 86:11
Teach me your way, Lord, that I may rely on your faithfulness; give me an undivided heart, that I may fear your name.

My best skill was that I was coachable. I was a sponge and aggressive to learn.
- Michael Jordan

YOU MUST ALWAYS

BE THE APPRENTICE.

EVEN WHEN YOU BECOME

{ THE MASTER... }

~ CHRISTOPHER CUMBY

If you are **not willing** to learn, no one can help you

If you are determined to learn, no one can stop you.
-Anonymous

Strength [strengkth]

the quality or state of being strong; bodily or mental power; vigor.

There is no denying that strength plays a key factor in your success as a wrestler. As soon as you tie up with your opponent in wrestling, you know if you are out-gunned from a physical aspect or not. Your opponent's physical strength in his grip, his legs, and his arms all become very evident from the starting whistle. That is why you need to dedicate yourself to strength training all year long. Weight training helps decrease the risk of injury, increase lean muscle mass, decrease body fat, increase bone density, improve mood, improve speed, improve strength and much more. If you are spending all of your time cutting weight, then you are missing out on your full potential. You should be lifting all season long. There is no substitute for strength on a wrestling mat. Strength can make up for areas where you lack in technique. I am a believer that technique ultimately wins matches, but strength is a great equalizer. Strength and endurance go hand in hand. These are both areas that you need to continue to work on in order to be a successful wrestler.

Strength is not only physical but mental as well. Maybe even more important than your physique is your mental fortitude or toughness. Again, your mind controls your body. If you allow your mind to quit or panic, your body will soon follow. If you are able to focus and calm your mind, your body will maintain its strength. Mental strength is about regulating your emotions, managing your thoughts, and behaving in a positive manner despite your circumstances. This is much easier said than done. This is developed through a pattern of healthy habits, hard work and commitment. Just like physical strength training, you have to embark on mental training to develop strength of mind. Do not waste your energy thinking about things that you cannot control. Worry causes mental exhaustion and allows negativity to creep into your mind which tears at the fabric of your mental toughness. Feeding your mind with positive thoughts and outcomes is much more productive in the development of mental strength. Get comfortable being uncomfortable. Experiencing failure or being in positions that you cannot control, usually puts you out of your comfort zone. When you are practicing, put yourself in positions that you don't feel like you are in control. If that means during practice that you give up a takedown or go to your back in the process, so be it. Be willing to learn from it so that you can improve and get comfortable in all positions even the uncomfortable ones. Developing both mental and physical strength is a work in progress. Each day requires purposeful effort on your part.

In addition to physical and mental strength, there is an area of spiritual strength that you need to develop and possess. This strength is more about your identity and recognizing who you are. Your identity cannot depend on whether you win or lose on the wrestling mat. It is about knowing that you have a greater purpose than just being a good wrestler. It is understanding your identity is in Christ. It is about relying and trusting in someone greater than yourself. It is about trusting God. Spiritual strength gives you the power you need to live a life of purpose and fulfillment. Wrestling is just something you do, your spiritual strength defines who you are.

Spiritual strength comes from trusting God despite your circumstances. It is realizing that your faith is bigger than your fears. Be willing to step out in your faith. Every step you take in faith is a step towards increased spiritual strength and growth. Every day is an opportunity to improve your physical, mental and spiritual strength. Be bold, be committed and be ready for the challenge.

Reflection: Where am I needing to improve my strength? Am I mentally, physically and spiritually strong?

Prayer: Lord, give me the strength to commit to training physically, mentally and spiritually. Help me to rely on You, Lord, for my strength so I can make much of You. Amen

Strength [strengkth]

the quality or state of being strong; bodily or mental power; vigor.

Philippians 4:13
I can do all this through him who gives me strength.

Ephesians 6:10
Finally, be strong in the Lord and in his mighty power.

Isaiah 40:31
but those who hope in the Lord will renew their strength. They will soar on wings like eagles; they will run and not grow weary, they will walk and not be faint.

Mark 12:30
Love the Lord your God with all your heart and with all your soul and with all your mind and with all your strength.

Romans 5:6
You see, at just the right time, when we were still powerless, Christ died for the ungodly.

2 Corinthians 12:9
But he said to me, "My grace is sufficient for you, for my power is made perfect in weakness." Therefore I will boast all the more gladly about my weaknesses, so that Christ's power may rest on me.

Deuteronomy 6:5
Love the Lord your God with all your heart and with all your soul and with all your strength.

Philippians 2:13
for it is God who works in you to will and to act in order to fulfill his good purpose.

Psalms 27:1
The Lord is my light and my salvation—whom shall I fear? The Lord is the stronghold of my life—of whom shall I be afraid?

Psalms 19:14
May these words of my mouth and this meditation of my heart be pleasing in your sight, Lord, my Rock and my Redeemer.

1 Timothy 1:12
I thank Christ Jesus our Lord, who has given me strength, that he considered me trustworthy, appointing me to his service.

1 Peter 4:11
If anyone speaks, they should do so as one who speaks the very words of God. If anyone serves, they should do so with the strength God provides, so that in all things God may be praised through Jesus Christ. To him be the glory and the power for ever and ever. Amen.

Psalms 18:2
The Lord is my rock, my fortress and my deliverer; my God is my rock, in whom I take refuge, my shield, and the horn of my salvation, my stronghold.

STRENGTH doesn't come from what you can do. It comes from OVERCOMING the things you thought you could not do

GOD GIVES HIS HARDEST FIGHTS FOR HIS STRONGEST SOLDIERS

KEEP THE FAITH AND KEEP GOING

"WITH A NEW DAY COMES NEW STRENGTH AND NEW THOUGHTS"

- ELEANOR ROOSEVELT

Focus [foh-kuh s]

cause to converge on a perceived point. to direct one's attention or efforts:

Have you ever been in the "zone" when you are out on the wrestling mat? The "zone" is a mental state that promotes peak performance. Being in this state of mind means that your mind is totally absorbed in the task at hand. Your thoughts and your actions are in perfect sync. It may feel like time slows down, the crowd and noise disappears, it feels as if your performance is on auto-pilot, you have a total sense of control of your body and mind and it as if your subconscious or instincts have completely taken over. Many top athletes speak of being in the "zone". But how do you get there? I would say it is largely a matter of focus. Your mental focus determines where you put your attention and your time.

Getting in the "zone" of optimal performance happens when your conscious mind is quiet allowing you to wrestle from the subconscious without distraction. Your conscious mind is what causes you to think and act voluntarily. Your subconscious mind causes you to react involuntarily. It is a reaction, many times based on "muscle memory" or "memory recall". Think about when you are first learning how to drive a car. You are driving the car "consciously", meaning every action is a "conscious" decision, like changing gears, applying brakes, turning and so on. After a few years of driving experience, you drive the car subconsciously. The feet and hands are doing their job and you are usually relaxed. You are not really thinking about how to do it or what to do. It is like driving to the same place that you have driven to 100 times without "consciously" navigating the way there. Your mind and body just knows the way.

I have experienced this same phenomenon over and over again on the wrestling mat. I have been so focused and in the "zone" during matches, that after wrestling a match, I have walked off the mat and did not remember what technique I used or what move I hit on them. My mind and body just reacted like it has done in the practice room time and time again. The key to getting in this state of mind is two-fold. First, you have to master your skills so that you can do them without thinking about how to do them. That takes practice and repetition. Second, you have to be able to focus and quiet your mind. The biggest distraction for a wrestler and the enemy of achieving "zone" performance is fear. It may be the fear of failure or the fear of getting it wrong or performing badly in the big-game or in front of your parents or in front of a big crowd. It may be the fear of your opponent or simply self-doubt. Whatever is distracting you, If you are unable to get your mind focused on the tasks at hand, it will be very difficult to get into the zone and reach your peak performance level. To reach the "zone" you need to be totally focused at your tasks at hand and then let your body and preparation take over. This breeds self-confidence, positivity and peace of mind.

We can learn a lot about focus in the scriptures. The bible elaborates on how you are to focus your life in general and how you are to deal with fear and distractions. Many verses talk about keeping your focus on God, having a focus on eternal life and the things above. You are to focus on the right path and the Lord's decrees. You are to set your mind and focus on Jesus and His grace and provisions for you. By focusing on the right things, that is how you have a purposeful and fulfilling life. There is a lot you can learn on and off the mat from God's Word and His emphasis on the importance of focus. So take captive every thought and do not fear. Focus on God's truth and you will discover all that He has planned for you.

Reflection: Am I letting fear prevent me from peak performance? Am I being distracted by circumstances rather than focusing on God's truths?

Prayer: Lord, Your ways are the best ways. Please help me focus on Your truths. Help me to lay aside my fears and trust in You and Your word. Thank You, Amen.

Focus [foh-kuh s]

cause to converge on a perceived point. *to direct one's attention or efforts:*

Colossians 3:2
Set your minds on things above, not on earthly things.

Proverbs 4:25
Let your eyes look straight ahead; fix your gaze directly before you.

Philippians 4:8
Finally, brothers and sisters, whatever is true, whatever is noble, whatever is right, whatever is pure, whatever is lovely, whatever is admirable—if anything is excellent or praiseworthy—think about such things.

2 Timothy 1:7
For the Spirit God gave us does not make us timid, but gives us power, love and self-discipline.

Hebrews 3:1
Therefore, holy brothers and sisters, who share in the heavenly calling, fix your thoughts on Jesus, whom we acknowledge as our apostle and high priest.

1 Peter 1:13
Therefore, with minds that are alert and fully sober, set your hope on the grace to be brought to you when Jesus Christ is revealed at his coming.

Hebrews 12:2
fixing our eyes on Jesus, the pioneer and perfecter of faith. For the joy set before him he endured the cross, scorning its shame, and sat down at the right hand of the throne of God.

Proverbs 23:19
Listen, my son, and be wise, and set your heart on the right path:

2 Corinthians 10:5
We demolish arguments and every pretension that sets itself up against the knowledge of God, and we take captive every thought to make it obedient to Christ.

Philippians 4:6-7
Do not be anxious about anything, but in every situation, by prayer and petition, with thanksgiving, present your requests to God. 7 And the peace of God, which transcends all understanding, will guard your hearts and your minds in Christ Jesus.

Proverbs 3:5-6
Trust in the Lord with all your heart and lean not on your own understanding;
in all your ways submit to him, and he will make your paths straight.

Colossians 3:16-17
Let the message of Christ dwell among you richly as you teach and admonish one another with all wisdom through psalms, hymns, and songs from the Spirit, singing to God with gratitude in your hearts. And whatever you do, whether in word or deed, do it all in the name of the Lord Jesus, giving thanks to God the Father through him.

STARVE
YOUR DISTRACTIONS
—
FEED
YOUR FOCUS

THE SUCCESSFUL WARRIOR IS THE AVERAGE MAN WITH LASER-LIKE FOCUS

-BRUCE LEE

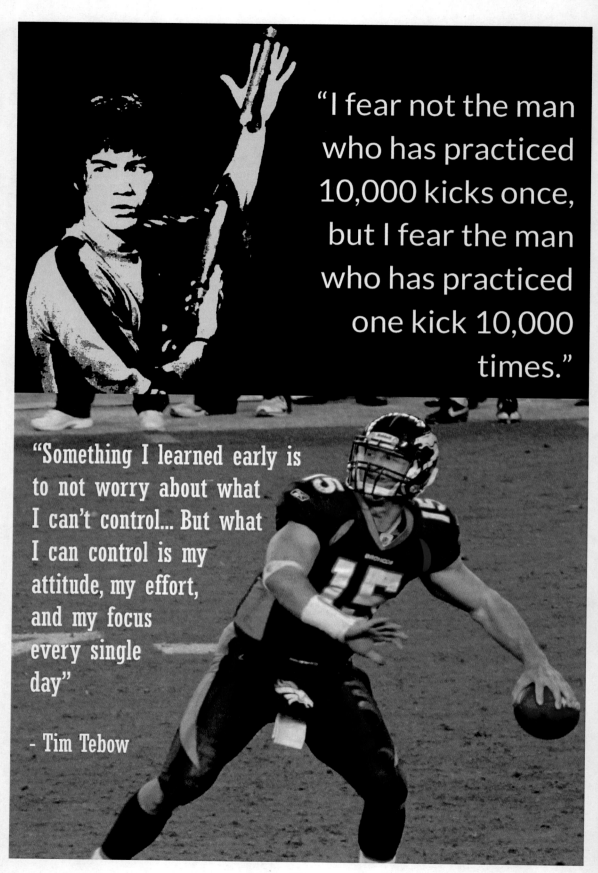

"I fear not the man who has practiced 10,000 kicks once, but I fear the man who has practiced one kick 10,000 times."

"Something I learned early is to not worry about what I can't control... But what I can control is my attitude, my effort, and my focus every single day"

- Tim Tebow

Respectful [ri-spekt-fuh l]

characterized by or showing politeness or deference: hold in esteem or honor

Respect and sportsmanship are one and the same. If you are showing good sportsmanship then you are being respectful. To respect others means to hold them in honor or esteem. It is about being others-focused rather than self-focused. It is imperative that you show respect to your teammates, your coaches, your parents, the referee and even your opponents By considering their thoughts, their feelings, and their positions and by controlling your actions through self-control, you are displaying respect. Showing a lack of respect reflects poorly on you, your family, your team, your school and your sport. You never know who is watching and who your actions are influencing. Respect and sportsmanship are extremely important character qualities. Let your performance on the wrestling mat and the way you conduct yourself speak louder than your words.

I have been in many wrestling gyms in my career and I have witnessed a lack of respect from all sides. Typically you see unsportsmanlike conduct when people become focused on themselves or when their emotions get involved. A referee's call did not go their way or they didn't get the outcome they wanted. A wrestler is losing so they give an unnecessary shove or do an illegal move to harm their opponent. You see people become vocal and start trash-talking, making inappropriate gestures to the crowds or blaming others for their failures. A wrestler with greater skills than their opponent taunts or showboats for the crowd. All of these are poor displays of character and shows a great level of disrespect. Showing a lack of respect does not change a loss to a win and it certainly does not make you a better person. It can also cause you to lose your dignity and the respect of others around you, which is much worse than any loss on your record from a wrestling match.

If you are struggling with knowing what is respectful, the golden rule of "whatever you wish that others would do to you, do also to them" should give you pretty solid guidelines. Shaking hands with your opponents whether you win or lose, showing concern for someone injured, accepting decisions by the referee even if you do not agree with them, encouraging your teammates and building them up even if they are less skilled than you, and listening and obeying your coaches or parents are all a good start. Controlling your tongue and refraining from trash talking, cheating or shaming and blaming others are also good examples of showing respect.

In the Bible the virtue of respect is conveyed in the words "honor" and "esteem". In the apostle Peter's first Epistle, he summarizes a teaching on respect in 1 Peter 2:17, "Show proper respect to everyone: Love the brotherhood of believers, fear God, honor the king." Essentially he encompasses four major areas of our lives on respect. You should show respect to everyone, no matter what race, gender, and status or skill level. Everyone means everyone and it is all-inclusive. You should also love your neighbors and respect other believers. You should respect and honor God with your thoughts and actions. And lastly, you need to respect author-ity whether that is the government, your coaches, your parents or anyone else that is placed in authority. If you want respect, you have to be willing to give it too.

Reflection: Have I displayed poor sportmanship in the past? Am I being respectful of my teammates, my coaches, the referees, my opponent and my sport?

Prayer: Lord, please help me to think of others first and honor them with my actions. Help me to show good sportsmanship even when I do not feel like it. Give me self-control and help me to be respectful to others. Amen.

"Sportsmanship for me is when a guy walks off the court and you really can't tell whether he won or lost, when he carries himself with pride either way."
- Jim Courier

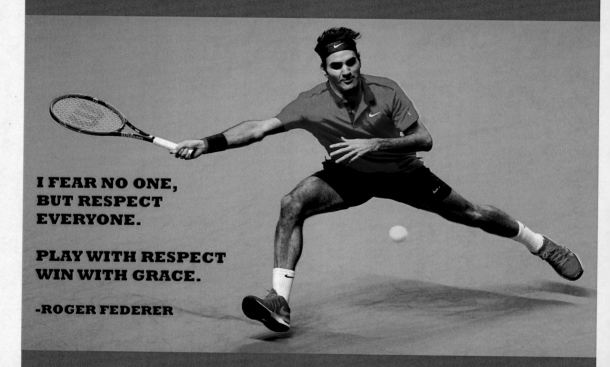

I FEAR NO ONE,
BUT RESPECT
EVERYONE.

PLAY WITH RESPECT
WIN WITH GRACE.

-ROGER FEDERER

When you win,
say nothing,
when you lose,
say less.

Respectful [ri-spekt-fuh l]

characterized by or showing politeness or deference: hold in esteem or honor

Romans 12:10
Love one another with brotherly affection. Outdo one another in showing honor.

Titus 2:7
Show yourself in all respects to be a model of good works, and in your teaching show integrity, dignity,

Ephesians 6:1-4
Children, obey your parents in the Lord, for this is right. "Honor your father and mother" (this is the first commandment with a promise), "that it may go well with you and that you may live long in the land." Fathers, do not provoke your children to anger, but bring them up in the discipline and instruction of the Lord.

Philippians 2:3-4
Do nothing from selfish ambition or conceit, but in humility count others more significant than yourselves. Let each of you look not only to his own interests, but also to the interests of others.

Matthew 7:12
So whatever you wish that others would do to you, do also to them, for this is the Law and the Prophets.

Exodus 20:12
Honor your father and your mother, that your days may be long in the land that the LORD your God is giving you.

1 Thessalonians 5:12-13
We ask you, brothers, to respect those who labor among you and are over you in the Lord and admonish you, and to esteem them very highly in love because of their work. Be at peace among yourselves.

Hebrews 13:7
Remember your leaders, those who spoke to you the word of God. Consider the outcome of their way of life, and imitate their faith.

Ephesians 5:33
However, let each one of you love his wife as himself, and let the wife see that she respects her husband.

Revelation 4:11
"Worthy are you, our Lord and God, to receive glory and honor and power, for you created all things, and by your will they existed and were created."

1 Peter 2:17
Honor everyone. Love the brotherhood. Fear God. Honor the emperor.

James 1:19
Know this, my beloved brothers: let every person be quick to hear, slow to speak, slow to anger;

Believe [bih-leev]

to have confidence in the truth, the existence, or the reliability of something; to have a conviction of belief

What is your WHY? Why do you do what you do? What is the purpose, cause, or belief that inspires you to do what you do? What is driving you? Why do you work out every day? Why do you get up early to put that extra work out in when you could just sleep in? Why do you skip the party that you really wanted to go to when you have a big match the next day? The whole purpose of understanding your WHY is really about uncovering what you truly want and believe. What you do proves what you believe. Your belief motivates your actions. Knowing your why creates in you this incredibly strong drive, power, energy and focus. A motivation that enables you to stand strong through tough times, to sacrifice your wants for what you know is the right things to do in order to achieve what you believe you can.

When I was an athlete, I truly believed I could win a national championship. It all started with the belief. Your "Why" affects what you do and how you do it. What you do proves what you believe. Would I really workout three times a day, sacrifice my social life during the wrestling season, skip the junk food and spend countless hours in the gym perfecting my skills if I didn't truly believe that I could accomplish my goal? I can tell you the answer is no. Many young athletes say they believe they will be a state or national champion but are not willing to put the work or effort in to prove their belief. If you truly believe in something, then what you do will always result in taking action to prove your why.

The same principle holds true in life. What is your WHY? What is your purpose in life? If you are a believer in Jesus Christ, than your purpose should be to make much of Him. In Exodus 9:16 it says, "I have raised you up for this very purpose, that I might show you my power and that my name might be proclaimed in all the earth". In Ephesians 2:10 the Bible says, "For we are God's workmanship, created in Christ Jesus to do good works, which God prepared in advance for us to do." Your "Why" or your purpose in life is to be used by God for His purpose so others may know Him. What you do proves what you believe. That is why if you say you are believer in Jesus, then your actions and the way we live your life should be different than those that do not believe. Your belief should affect your actions. You don't change your actions in order to earn God's acceptance, you change your actions because He first loved you and now you get to love others. The fruits of the spirit are not just superficial actions that are mustered up on your own strength, they are an outpouring of who you are because of your belief in Jesus Christ. It is out of your thanksgiving for God's grace and forgiveness that you now have the opportunity to share God's love with others so that they can come to know Him too. Your "Why" and what you believe, truly affects what you do.

You were placed on this earth with a purpose, God's purpose. That purpose is to glorify Him in everything you do and to love and serve the people around you. What that looks like for each individual may be different, but it is still the driving force behind what it means to be a believer in Jesus Christ. God can use you in a mighty way to reach others for His name. Maybe it is reaching other's through the platform of the sport of wrestling or maybe through your community involvement or your job or your hobbies. Whatever it is you do, do it for His glory not because you have to, but because you want to and you get the opportunity to. When you truly believe in something, it will always produce an action. Know your WHY.

Reflection: Are my actions proving what I believe? Am I making much of Him or trying to make much of Me? Do I truly believe what I say I believe?

Prayer: Lord, thank You for Your grace and your forgiveness. Help me to bring glory to You through the way I live my life and to make much of You so others may know You. Amen.

Believe [bih-leev]

to have confidence in the truth, the existence, or the reliability of something; to have a conviction of belief

John 14:12-14
Very truly I tell you, whoever believes in me will do the works I have been doing, and they will do even greater things than these, because I am going to the Father. And I will do whatever you ask in my name, so that the Father may be glorified in the Son. You may ask me for anything in my name, and I will do it.

John 3:16
For God so loved the world that he gave his one and only Son, that whoever believes in him shall not perish but have eternal life.

Mark 16:15-16
He said to them, "Go into all the world and preach the gospel to all creation. Whoever believes and is baptized will be saved, but whoever does not believe will be condemned.

John 14:1
Do not let your hearts be troubled. You believe in God[a]; believe also in me.

James 2:22
You see that his faith and his actions were working together, and his faith was made complete by what he did.

Colossians 3:17
And whatever you do, whether in word or deed, do it all in the name of the Lord Jesus, giving thanks to God the Father through him.

John 1:12
Yet to all who did receive him, to those who believed in his name, he gave the right to become children of God

Romans 4:3
What does Scripture say? "Abraham believed God, and it was credited to him as righteousness."

John 14:12
Very truly I tell you, whoever believes in me will do the works I have been doing, and they will do even greater things than these, because I am going to the Father.

Matthew 28:19
Therefore go and make disciples of all nations, baptizing them in the name of the Father and of the Son and of the Holy Spirit

Ephesians 1:13
And you also were included in Christ when you heard the message of truth, the gospel of your salvation. When you believed, you were marked in him with a seal, the promised Holy Spirit

John 11:40
Then Jesus said, "Did I not tell you that if you believe, you will see the glory of God?"

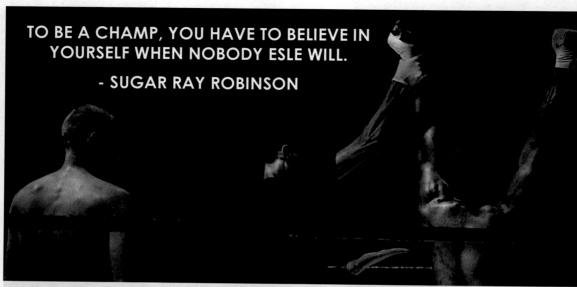

TO BE A CHAMP, YOU HAVE TO BELIEVE IN YOURSELF WHEN NOBODY ESLE WILL.
- SUGAR RAY ROBINSON

"Faith is to believe what you do not see; the reward of this faith is to see what you believe."

Saint Augustine

You are what you believe yourself to be.

Paulo Coelho

Patient [pey-shuh nt]

able to accept or tolerate delays, problems, or suffering without becoming annoyed or anxious.

You live in a society that emphasizes instant gratification. You want instant coffee, instant information at your finger tips, instant online movie rentals, instant fast food, instant delivery shipped right to your door and instant responses on text messaging and emails. It is no wonder that you also want instant success and results. Your life and the technology around you has fed your hunger for instant gratification but the reality is that it has also made you extremely impatient. When everything is going your way, patience is easy to demonstrate. The true test of patience comes when adversity strikes and your best laid plans are changed. When it comes to athletics, rarely does success happen immediately. It takes a lot of hard work, dedication, failures and perseverance. Success is often a function of time and effort. Becoming a successful athlete and developing the skill set needed to do so is not a sprint, it is a marathon.

Patience is a vital character trait for your athletic endeavors and your life. Patience is the ability and willingness to suppress restlessness, frustration and annoyance when you are confronted with delays or setbacks. A patient athlete is able to display composure, poise, perseverance, self-control and diligence in their performance to make the right decisions at the right moments. They are able to relax and maintain a positive attitude despite their circumstances. Impatience causes anxiety, tension and frustration. You must prepare for the unexpected because things are not always going to go your way or as you have planned. You must accept the twist and turns and unexpected things that happen on the wrestling mat and maintain your poise. A patient athlete is confident and is able to overcome doubt, worry and fear.

You need to approach life with the same attitude and patience. It is not a matter of if you will face setbacks, rather a matter of when and how often. You must recognize setbacks as temporary. The natural response when you do not get the results or response you want is to get impatient which leads to stress, anger and frustration. Thank God that you are no longer in bondage to a "natural response" because you are new creation in Christ. The Bible praises patience as a fruit of the Spirit that should be produced for all followers of Christ. Patience reveals your faith in God's timing, His omnipotence, and His love. You must recognize God's power and goodness and trust Him in order to truly develop patience.

How do you develop this type of patience? First, you must be thankful for God's provisions and blessings in your life. Even in the darkest of days, there is always something to be thankful for. Second, you must keep in mind your purpose. That purpose is to make much of God. Sometimes, God may allow difficult situations in your life so that you can be a witness to others. Other times, He allows trials to build your character. By remembering your purpose, you can endure trials. Lastly, you must remember God's promises. There are over 7,000 promises in the Bible. God promises that He will give you peace, joy, love, help, forgiveness and eternal life just to name a few. Cling to God's truths in times of trials and you can endure those trials with great patience. You want instant gratification and instant success with abundant victories and perfection in all you do. However, the reality of success is more about emphasizing character, developing your abilities and keeping winning and losing in their proper perspective. I encourage you to focus on and trust the process, embrace the grind and the results will take care of themselves in due time. Be patient and continue to trust God.

Reflection: Am I trusting God or allowing my circumstances to dictate my attitude?

Prayer: Lord, help me to trust You, to be thankful and to be patient in my circumstances. Lord, help me to learn patience as I wait for Your answers. Thank You for assuring me that Your plans for me are good. Amen

Patient [pey-shuh nt]

able to accept or tolerate delays, problems, or suffering without becoming annoyed or anxious.

Romans 12:12
Be joyful in hope, patient in affliction, faithful in prayer.

Romans 8:25
But if we hope for what we do not yet have, we wait for it patiently.

Galatians 6:9
Let us not become weary in doing good, for at the proper time we will reap a harvest if we do not give up.

Psalm 37:7-9
Be still before the Lord and wait patiently for him; do not fret when people succeed in their ways, when they carry out their wicked schemes. Refrain from anger and turn from wrath; do not fret— it leads only to evil. For those who are evil will be destroyed, but those who hope in the Lord will inherit the land.

Philippians 4:6
Do not be anxious about anything, but in every situation, by prayer and petition, with thanksgiving, present your requests to God.

Jeremiah 29:11
For I know the plans I have for you," declares the Lord, "plans to prosper you and not to harm you, plans to give you hope and a future.

Ephesians 4:2
Be completely humble and gentle; be patient, bearing with one another in love.

1 Corinthians 13:4
Love is patient, love is kind. It does not envy, it does not boast, it is not proud.

1 Peter 2:19-23
For it is commendable if someone bears up under the pain of unjust suffering because they are conscious of God. But how is it to your credit if you receive a beating for doing wrong and endure it? But if you suffer for doing good and you endure it, this is commendable before God. To this you were called, because Christ suffered for you, leaving you an example, that you should follow in his steps."He committed no sin, and no deceit was found in his mouth." When they hurled their insults at him, he did not retaliate; when he suffered, he made no threats. Instead, he entrusted himself to him who judges justly

Romans 5:3-4
Not only so, but we also glory in our sufferings, because we know that suffering produces perseverance; perseverance, character; and character, hope.

James 1:19
My dear brothers and sisters, take note of this: Everyone should be quick to listen, slow to speak and slow to become angry,

James 5:8
You too, be patient and stand firm, because the Lord's coming is near.

PATIENCE
IS NOT THE
ABILITY TO WAIT
BUT HOW YOU
ACT WHILE YOU'RE
WAITING

- JOYCE MEYER

"Patience is bitter, but its fruit is sweet."

- Aristotle

"Have PATIENCE All things are DIFFICULT before they BECOME easy."

- Saadi

Determination [dih-tur-muh-ney-shuh n]

the quality of being resolute; firmness of purpose.

Every goal that you set must always be met with the determination to reach it. Your determination is what keeps you focused on attaining your goals despite setbacks, resistance and failures. It is what continues to drive you toward your purpose or goal. It is what allows you to not be distracted or discouraged in your pursuit. Determination gives you the resolve to keep going in spite of the roadblocks that lay before you. It requires persistence and perseverance to overcome barriers that may hold you back. To reach your goal you must first believe in what you are doing and believe that you can reach that goal. Second, you must take action to achieve it. Lastly, you must have determination to STAY in action until you accomplish the goal.

Everything in this world seems to try to bring you down. You hit hardships, challenges and roadblocks throughout life. There will be times when you will be discouraged and want to quit and give up. The one quality that will guarantee your success is your determination to refuse to quit. After all, how can you possibly fail, if you never give up? Adversity and discouragement are inevitable realities no matter how well you plan or try to execute a plan. Adversity is a great teacher to develop your inner character. Thomas Edison was one of the world's great inventors. Edison once said, "I have not failed. I've just found 10,000 ways that won't work. Our greatest weakness lies in giving up. The most certain way to succeed is always to try just one more time. Many of life's failures are people who did not realize how close they were to success when they gave up." Edison was determined to succeed. Your determination directs your decisions.

There are many examples of men in the Bible that displayed great determination. If you read about Daniel in Daniel 6, Daniel determined to do what was right despite the consequences and leave the outcome to God. Daniel's life was surely in danger if he decided to continue his prayer to God each day. Yet, Daniel was determined to honor God and trust Him alone with the outcome of his life. Daniel did not choose to do what was easiest, he was determined to do what was right and God was faithful to protect Daniel in the lion's den for his faith. Another example of great determination can be found in the story of the paralytic in Mark 2. Four men carried their paralyzed friend to a home where they knew Jesus was teaching. They were determined to get their paralyzed friend to Jesus because they believed Jesus could heal him. When they arrived at the home where Jesus was teaching, the house was full. The crowd was too large and they could not get in. Undeterred and determined to help their friend, these men carried their friend to the roof of the house and then dug through the roof to create an opening where they lowered their friend down to Jesus. Their determination to not give up resulted in their friend being healed and caused people to praise God. Obstacles may seem insurmountable but being determined to continue on anyway and trust God is the difference in success or failure. That was the case for Joshua and the battle at Jericho. Joshua faced a city that was heavily fortified and virtually impenetrable. God revealed to Joshua a plan that would enable them to conquer the city but it was illogical and did not make sense from a human perspective. Joshua faced ridicule from his peers and self-doubt but was determined to obey and trust God and do it God's way. Joshua's strong faith in God led him to obey God and the wall came down just as God said it would. Be determined to see whatever it is you are facing through to the end. Don't allow setback, obstacles or people's discouragement stop you from attaining your goals and finishing what you started. Be determined to having victory in your walk with Jesus.

Reflection: Am I determined to follow Jesus no matter what obstacles are in my way? Am I giving up on something that I have started?

Prayer: Lord, please restore my determination to do what is right and to keep moving forward. I pray that You strengthen my resolve to finish well. Amen.

Determination [dih-tur-muh-ney-shuh n]

the quality of being resolute; firmness of purpose.

2 Timothy 4:7
I have fought the good fight, I have finished the race, I have kept the faith.

2 Chronicles 15:7
But as for you, be strong and do not give up, for your work will be rewarded.

Psalm 44:18
Our hearts had not turned back; our feet had not strayed from your path.

Psalm 119:10
I seek you with all my heart; do not let me stray from your commands.

1 Corinthians 9:24-27
Do you not know that in a race all the runners run, but only one gets the prize? Run in such a way as to get the prize. Everyone who competes in the games goes into strict training. They do it to get a crown that will not last, but we do it to get a crown that will last forever. Therefore I do not run like someone running aimlessly; I do not fight like a boxer beating the air. No, I strike a blow to my body and make it my slave so that after I have preached to others, I myself will not be disqualified for the prize.

Philippians 4:13
I can do all this through him who gives me strength.

Psalms 27:14
Wait for the Lord; be strong and take heart and wait for the Lord.

1 Thessalonians 3:8
For now we really live, since you are standing firm in the Lord.

2 Thessalonians 3:13
And as for you, brothers and sisters, never tire of doing what is good.

Ephesians 6:11
Put on the full armor of God, so that you can take your stand against the devil's schemes.

2 Corinthians 4:8-11
We are hard pressed on every side, but not crushed; perplexed, but not in despair; persecuted, but not abandoned; struck down, but not destroyed. We always carry around in our body the death of Jesus, so that the life of Jesus may also be revealed in our body. For we who are alive are always being given over to death for Jesus' sake, so that his life may also be revealed in our mortal body

Ephesians 6:16
In addition to all this, take up the shield of faith, with which you can extinguish all the flaming arrows of the evil one.

Isaiah 8:9-11
Prepare for battle, and be shattered! Devise your strategy, but it will be thwarted; propose your plan, but it will not stand, for God is with us

Some people **Succeed** because they are **DESTINED** but most because they are **DETERMINED**

- unknown

I am **too positive** to be doubtful,

too optimistic to be fearful,

and **too determined** to be defeated.

Thankful [thangk-fuh l]

feeling or expressing gratitude; appreciative.

You may wonder, how does being thankful make me a better wrestler or athlete? I would say that being thankful may be one of the most important characteristics a person can possess. Sometimes in your athletic pursuits, you get so focused on the failures that come with trying to succeed that it consumes you and controls your thinking. You start to focus on the shortfalls, the stress, the pressure, the worry and the frustrations and you lose focus and perspective on the things that are important. You create a negative mindset which then affects your overall attitude and ultimately your performance. Thankfulness is simply recognizing your blessings and the things that you should appreciate and be grateful for.

Being thankful helps fight all of the negativity and puts losses and setbacks into proper perspective. Thankfulness develops a mindset that nothing has the ability to compromise your contentment. It enables you to look outside of yourself and focus on others. It keeps you humble, grateful, appreciative and positive. Your life is often tainted by your own skewed perspective which is typically not a true reflection of reality. You can make a big deal about small things that have very little bearing on the big picture of your life. If you can slow down and reflect on all the things that you truly are thankful for, then you can have a better and clearer perspective of the things that are truly important. The truth is that if you are able to compete in sports, then you have talents and abilities that many less fortunate people may only dream of having. There are many children, teenagers and young adults who will never have the opportunity to step on a wrestling mat and even have the chance to compete or have the opportunity to have their hand raised in victory. They are busy fighting a disease, disability, hunger, poverty or abuse. Remember that you are blessed just to be able to compete and that your gifts and talents comes from God. Always be thankful and keep life in the proper perspective.

When you are thankful, your focus moves off your selfish desires and off the pain of your current circumstances. Expressing thankfulness helps you remember that God is in control. It reminds you of the bigger picture, that you belong to God, and that you have been blessed with much to be thankful for. It allows you to reflect and be thankful for your family, your parents, your friends, your talents, your abilities, your health, your coaches, your teammates, your opportunities, your job, your safety and so much more. In fact, you can even be thankful for your pain and hardships because they can teach you and lead you to more growth than you would have experienced without them. Being thankful is a choice. It is not a feeling. You can be thankful even when you do not feel like it. Even when the world around you is not going how you had hoped or planned, you can be thankful for God's eternal blessings. As a believer in Jesus, it is important that you keep an eternal perspective. You must know that even when this life fades away, you are blessed through your relationship with Jesus that leads to eternal life. So even in the darkest days, you can choose to trust God and know that He is good, He is righteous and He loves you deeply. You can be assured if you have put your faith and trust in Him alone, that your spirit is secure with Him for all eternity. That is always something you can be thankful for. Your life is not defined by your performance on a wrestling mat. Make sure you look a the bigger picture and keep the important things in life in the proper perspective. Be thankful for your blessings.

Reflection: Have I allowed my circumstances to dictate my attitude? Has negativity and worry controlled my thoughts? Do I have a thankful heart or am I consumed with bitterness?

Prayer: Lord, please help remind me of all of the blessings that You have given me. Please help me to have a thankful heart and remove the bitterness that has consumed me. Lord, please forgive me for not recognizing Your grace and blessings. Amen.

THERE IS
Always, Always
Something TO BE
Thankful FOR

"TALENT IS GOD GIVEN. BE HUMBLE. FAME IS MAN-GIVEN. BE GRATEFUL. CONCEIT IS SELF-GIVEN. BE CAREFUL."
- JOHN WOODEN

Thankful [thangk-fuh l]

feeling or expressing gratitude; appreciative.

1 Thessalonians 5:18
give thanks in all circumstances; for this is God's will for you in Christ Jesus.

Psalms 107:1
Give thanks to the Lord, for he is good; his love endures forever.

Ephesians 5:20
always giving thanks to God the Father for everything, in the name of our Lord Jesus Christ.

Colossians 3:15-17
Let the peace of Christ rule in your hearts, since as members of one body you were called to peace. And be thankful. Let the message of Christ dwell among you richly as you teach and admonish one another with all wisdom through psalms, hymns, and songs from the Spirit, singing to God with gratitude in your hearts. And whatever you do, whether in word or deed, do it all in the name of the Lord Jesus, giving thanks to God the Father through him.

James 1:17
Every good and perfect gift is from above, coming down from the Father of the heavenly lights, who does not change like shifting shadows.

Philippians 4:6
Do not be anxious about anything, but in every situation, by prayer and petition, with thanksgiving, present your requests to God.

Psalms 106:1
Praise the Lord. Give thanks to the Lord, for he is good; his love endures forever.

Psalms 105:1
Give praise to the Lord, proclaim his name; make known among the nations what he has done.

Colossians 3:15
Let the peace of Christ rule in your hearts, since as members of one body you were called to peace. And be thankful.

Colossians 4:2
Devote yourselves to prayer, being watchful and thankful.

Psalms 118:1
Give thanks to the Lord, for he is good; his love endures forever.

Colossians 3:17
And whatever you do, whether in word or deed, do it all in the name of the Lord Jesus, giving thanks to God the Father through him.

Romans 1:21
For although they knew God, they neither glorified him as God nor gave thanks to him, but their thinking became futile and their foolish hearts were darkened.

Thankful [thangk-fuh l]

feeling or expressing gratitude; appreciative.

1 Corinthians 15:57
But thanks be to God! He gives us the victory through our Lord Jesus Christ.

2 Corinthians 2:14-15
But thanks be to God, who always leads us as captives in Christ's triumphal procession and uses us to spread the aroma of the knowledge of him everywhere. For we are to God the pleasing aroma of Christ among those who are being saved and those who are perishing.

Colossians 1:12
and giving joyful thanks to the Father, who has qualified you to share in the inheritance of his holy people in the kingdom of light.

Ephesians 5:4
Nor should there be obscenity, foolish talk or coarse joking, which are out of place, but rather thanksgiving.

Revelation 11:17
We give thanks to you, Lord God Almighty, the One who is and who was, because you have taken your great power and have begun to reign.

Philippians 4:4-7
Rejoice in the Lord always. I will say it again: Rejoice! Let your gentleness be evident to all. The Lord is near. Do not be anxious about anything, but in every situation, by prayer and petition, with thanksgiving, present your requests to God. And the peace of God, which transcends all understanding, will guard your hearts and your minds in Christ Jesus.

Psalms 103:2-5
Praise the Lord, my soul, and forget not all his benefits—who forgives all your sins and heals all your diseases, who redeems your life from the pit and crowns you with love and compassion, who satisfies your desires with good things so that your youth is renewed like the eagle's.

Isaiah 12:4-5
In that day you will say: "Give praise to the Lord, proclaim his name; make known among the nations what he has done, and proclaim that his name is exalted. Sing to the Lord, for he has done glorious things; let this be known to all the world.

Psalm 100:4
Enter his gates with thanksgiving and his courts with praise; give thanks to him and praise his name.

Psalm 95:2
Let us come before him with thanksgiving and extol him with music and song.

1 Chronicles 29:13
Now, our God, we give you thanks, and praise your glorious name.

Psalms 30:12
that my heart may sing your praises and not be silent. Lord my God, I will praise you forever.

Discipline [dis-uh-plin]

activity, exercise, or a regimen that develops or improves a skill; training. Punishment inflicted by way of correction and training; to bring to a state of obedience by training.

If you have ever set a goal for yourself, then you know it takes discipline to achieve it. Discipline can be self-imposed or imposed from someone else. Both are essential when it comes to being a successful athlete. Wrestling is a sport that combines both mental and physical discipline in order to reach the pinnacle of the sport. Discipline is never fun, but it is necessary in order for you to achieve your goals.

Self-discipline is the conscious choices that you make over and over again in order to form a habit or a lifestyle. Discipline is living and making choices in a way that aligns with your goals. This type of discipline includes choices regarding your conditioning, healthy eating, strength training, stress management, visualization, learning, sleeping habits, work ethic, and training intensity. So essentially, every aspect of wrestling involves some form of discipline. To possess discipline you have to be able to make decisions, take appropriate actions and execute your plan despite any obstacles, discomfort and pain that comes your way. To be successful, you must cultivate a mindset that you are ruled by your deliberate choices rather than by your emotions or outside influences. Discipline is dragging yourself out of bed for an early run or going to the gym for the third time in a day not because you want to, but because you need to. It is going to bed early even though you want to go out late with your friends or watch a TV show. It is eating a salad when the rest of your family is eating pizza and wings. It is choosing to do the things that you know you need to do over the things that you want to do. No personal success, achievement or goal can be realized without self-discipline. Discipline is being able to turn down instant gratification in favor of gaining the long-term satisfaction and fulfillment from achieving higher and more meaningful goals.

The second form of discipline may be imposed on you from an outside source like a coach or a parent. This type of discipline is also very important because it corrects your behavior or your training. This type of discipline if applied properly can help athletes accept personal responsibility, team accountability, resolve confrontations, break bad habits and improve athletic skills. If done properly by a coach or parent, discipline tends to produce positive results not negative ones. Discipline is essential for any effective athlete or team.

Discipline in both forms are not only essential in sports but in life. You need self-discipline in your Christian walk to control your impulses, emotions, and desires in order to resist temptations. You need discipline and instruction from others and God in order to correct your thinking and change your behavior in a way that honors God. The Bible teaches that discipline is not only an important characteristic of a believer but it is necessary and essential for growth. Both forms of discipline are needed in order to reflect Christ in your thoughts and actions so that others may see Jesus through your life and the way you live it.

Reflection: Are there areas of my life I need self-discipline? Have I created a pattern of disobedience in my life? Do I need someone to speak discipline into my life to correct my thinking and my behavior?

Prayer: Lord, I know discipline is hard but I also know that it is important in order to grow spiritually. Lord, give me the strength to have self-discipline to avoid temptation and to rely on You. Help me to receive discipline with an open heart and open mind so that I can reflect You to others in a glorifying way. Amen

DISCIPLINE IS DOING WHAT NEEDS TO BE DONE, EVEN WHEN YOU DON'T WANT TO DO IT.

Discipline is the bridge between goals and accomplishment.

Jim Rohn

DISCIPLINE IS JUST CHOOSING BETWEEN WHAT YOU WANT NOW AND WHAT YOU WANT MOST.

Discipline [dis-uh-plin]

activity, exercise, or a regimen that develops or improves a skill; training.

1 Corinthians 9:27
No, I strike a blow to my body and make it my slave so that after I have preached to others, I myself will not be disqualified for the prize.

Hebrews 12:11
No discipline seems pleasant at the time, but painful. Later on, however, it produces a harvest of righteousness and peace for those who have been trained by it.

Titus 1:8
Rather, he must be hospitable, one who loves what is good, who is self-controlled, upright, holy and disciplined.

1 Timothy 4:7
Have nothing to do with godless myths and old wives' tales; rather, train yourself to be godly.

Hebrews 5:8
Son though he was, he learned obedience from what he suffered

Discipline [dis-uh-plin]

Punishment inflicted by way of correction and training; to bring to a state of obedience by training.

Proverbs 12:1
Whoever loves discipline loves knowledge, but whoever hates correction is stupid.

Proverbs 13:24
Whoever spares the rod hates their children, but the one who loves their children is careful to discipline them

Hebrews 12:5-6
And have you completely forgotten this word of encouragement that addresses you as a father addresses his son? It says,"My son, do not make light of the Lord's discipline, and do not lose heart when he rebukes you, because the Lord disciplines the one he loves, and he chastens everyone he accepts as his son."

Proverbs 3:11-12
My son, do not despise the Lord's discipline,and do not resent his rebuke, because the Lord disciplines those he loves, as a father the son he delights in.

Proverbs 6:23
For this command is a lamp, this teaching is a light, and correction and instruction are the way to life,

Proverbs 13:1
A wise son heeds his father's instruction, but a mocker does not respond to rebukes

Deuteronomy 8:5
Know then in your heart that as a man disciplines his son, so the Lord your God disciplines you.

MOTIVATION

MAY GET YOU STARTED
BUT IT TAKES

DISCIPLINE

TO KEEP YOU GOING. *Bonnie Pfiester*

SUFFER
THE PAIN OF
DISCIPLINE
OR
SUFFER
THE PAIN OF
REGRET

Passionate [pash-uh-nit]

expressing, showing, or marked by intense or strong feeling or desire: vehement in spirit

I have seen many talented wrestlers that were very skilled in the sport of wrestling but their heart just wasn't in it. Their talents and their desires were not aligned. They showed up to practice and the workouts, but wrestling was just something they did because they were good at it rather than something they loved. They had no hunger or desire to seek excellence or greatness. It is true that you can be good at something and still have no passion for it. But, in order to reach the next level of your sport, your heart, your head and your body all have to work in the same direction and that comes down to being passionate about what you do.

Passion is the energy that keeps you going, that keeps you excited, motivated and filled with anticipation to get up in the morning to pursue your dreams. Passionate people are positive and authentic because they are doing what they love to do. Their skills and talents are aligned with their hearts to work on whatever it is they are striving for. Having passion for what you are doing is extremely important in order to reach your full potential. If you are approaching your goals, your workouts, your job, or your life by just going through the motions then you are probably suffering from a lack of joy and happiness in your life. Passion creates the desire to motivate you and allows you to deal with frustration and adversity properly. This drive must come from within you. It is understanding and believing in your purpose. Passion gives you a reason to keep learning, keep trying and to keep working towards your goals. Without passion, you may experience depression, fatigue, stress, frustration, self-pity and a lack of motivation. Your passion provides you with the willingness to persevere with your training, to endure discomfort and stress, and to make sacrifices with your time and energy as you move closer toward realizing your goal. You need to love your sport and have a burning desire to be the best version of yourself you can be. That does not mean you are going to like or enjoy the process along the way but your passion enables you to push yourself to do what has to be done. It keeps you hungry and emotionally connected to your goals.

You can lose your passion and walk through your life going through the motions or just existing. You get consumed with the daily routines and stop doing the things that you love and the things that you are passionate about. This can also occur in your walk with Jesus. You can allow your walk to become stale and routine. As a believer, you are called to be passionate about Christ. You may ask, "How do I get a passion for Jesus?" The answer is in Deuteronomy 6:4-5 when Jesus reveals the greatest commandment, "to love the Lord your God with all your heart and with all your soul and with all your strength." In other words, to have a true and authentic love of the Lord and pursue Him with your whole being. To do that, you must know God and pursue Him through His word and prayer. Then, you can figure out what you stand for, identify your purpose and pursue it with a passion. Be purposeful, be passionate and be authentic in your walk with Jesus. Love what you do and do what you love. Your passion for Christ can attract and lead others to salvation.

Reflection: What do I love to do? Where is my passion? Am I doing what I love or am I getting caught up in routines? Can I use my passions to reach others for Christ?

Prayer: Lord, thank You for my talents. I pray that my talents can align with my passions. I pray that You can use my gifts to reach others for You. Help me to passionately seek my goals and pursue You. Amen.

Passionate [pash-uh-nit]

expressing, showing, or marked by intense or strong feeling or desire: vehement in spirit

Philippians 3:7-8
But whatever were gains to me I now consider loss for the sake of Christ. What is more, I consider everything a loss because of the surpassing worth of knowing Christ Jesus my Lord, for whose sake I have lost all things.

Luke 24:32
They asked each other, "Were not our hearts burning within us while he talked with us on the road and opened the Scriptures to us?"

John 17:26
I have made you[a] known to them, and will continue to make you known in order that the love you have for me may be in them and that I myself may be in them."

Colossians 3:23
Whatever you do, work at it with all your heart, as working for the Lord, not for human masters,

Psalm 73:25-26
Whom have I in heaven but you? And earth has nothing I desire besides you. My flesh and my heart may fail, but God is the strength of my heart and my portion forever.

1 Corinthians 9:24
Do you not know that in a race all the runners run, but only one gets the prize? Run in such a way as to get the prize.

Psalm 84:2
My soul yearns, even faints, for the courts of the Lord; my heart and my flesh cry out for the living God.

Matthew 6:21
For where your treasure is, there your heart will be also.

1 Corinthians 10:31
So whether you eat or drink or whatever you do, do it all for the glory of God.

Deuteronomy 6:4-5
Hear, O Israel: The Lord our God, the Lord is one. Love the Lord your God with all your heart and with all your soul and with all your strength.

Matthew 22:37-38
Jesus replied: "'Love the Lord your God with all your heart and with all your soul and with all your mind.'[a] 38 This is the first and greatest commandment.

Mark 12:30
Love the Lord your God with all your heart and with all your soul and with all your mind and with all your strength.

Matthew 5:6
Blessed are those who hunger and thirst for righteousness, for they will be filled.

The only way
to do great
work is to love
what you do.

-Steve Jobs

"EVERY GREAT DREAM BEGINS WITH A DREAMER.
ALWAYS REMEMBER, YOU HAVE WITHIN YOU
THE STRENGTH, THE PATIENCE, AND THE
PASSION TO REACH FOR THE STARS TO
CHANGE THE WORLD."

- HARRIET TUBMAN

"You must be passionate, you must
dedicate yourself, and you must
be relentless in the pursuit of your
goals. If you do, you will be
successful."

- Steve Garvey

Endurance [en-doo r-uh ns]

the ability or strength to continue or last, especially despite fatigue, stress, or other adverse conditions; stamina:

Your lungs are burning as your chest is heaving and grasping for air. Your legs feel like rubber and concrete at the same time. Your forearms are hard as a rock and you can barely pull yourself off the mat to stand up. You look up at the clock and you are down by 1 with 20 seconds to go. Your mind says take a shot but your body has nothing left. How can you be so exhausted? How can your body seemingly shut down in such a short period of time? Welcome to the sport of wrestling. Wrestling is one of the most physically demanding sports on the planet. It has the ability to physically drain your body of strength in just a few short minutes. The only way to combat this fatigue is by training and improving your endurance. Wrestling matches can be grueling, so endurance is extremely important for wrestlers. If an athlete lacks this attribute, he or she will quickly run out of energy. Wrestling requires an athlete to sustain high levels of energy very quickly and recover in a very short period of time. In order to be successful, you have to train your muscles, your lungs, your heart and your mind to endure this extreme demand. Wrestling is a series of sudden, explosive attacks and counterattacks that are executed on a repeated basis for duration up to 6 or 7 minutes. Your level of endurance or conditioning is many times the difference from winning and losing against an equally skilled opponent. A strong, well-conditioned cardiovascular system will enable your body to receive more oxygen and a higher volume of blood from your heart. This in turn improves your energy production to meet the demands of a wrestling match. Often times you hear coaches say that a wrestler "ran out of gas" or that he needs to "get in shape". This has everything to do with the wrestler's endurance. In order to compete on the highest level, you have to have endurance and maintain a high quality of work in the face of fatigue. A wrestler must train his endurance on many levels. A great wrestler must develop and train their aerobic, anaerobic, speed, power and strength endurance in order to have success in wrestling. Without endurance, even the most skilled wresters will fail. You must have endurance to overcome the pain and fatigue so that you can finish the match strong.

In the same way, you must have endurance in life. You must find the strength and stamina to bear the pain of your trials in order to finish strong in your walk with Christ. You must be able to endure in all circumstances to finish what you started no matter what adversity comes your way. You may be tired, stressed, or burnt out with life at times but it is your endurance that will get you through it. Enduring is difficult, but God does not want you to give up. God wants you to remember that you are not running this race alone. In Deuteronomy 31:6 it says, "The Lord your God goes with you; he will never leave you nor forsake you." We must remember that endurance produces character and character produces hope. Hope allows you to approach problems with a mindset and strategy that has a pathway to success. In your Christian walk, that pathway to success is your hope in God's promise that if you believe in Jesus, then you will spend eternity with Him. Therefore, you endure whatever comes your way here on earth because the ultimate prize is an eternal one. By enduring your trials here on earth, you can witness to others so they may also know Christ. Just like on the wrestling mat, you must train your mind and your body to improve your endurance. By focusing on Christ and trusting in Him, you can endure the trials of this life. The level of your endurance is equal to the level of trust and faith that you place in God. If you trust God and keep an eternal perspective by recognizing that He is in control, then you can endure any trials you face on earth.

Reflection: Am I enduring well with my life? Am I "out of shape" when it comes to my faith and walk with God? Do I need to improve on my level of endurance?

Prayer: Lord, thank You for Your promises and the hope that You give me. Help me to train my mind and body on Jesus so that I can endure these trials I am facing well. Amen.

Endurance [en-doo r-uh ns]

the ability or strength to continue or last, especially despite fatigue, stress, or other adverse conditions; stamina:

Romans 5:3-4
More than that, we rejoice in our sufferings, knowing that suffering produces endurance, and endurance produces character, and character produces hope,

James 1:12
Blessed is the man who remains steadfast under trial, for when he has stood the test he will receive the crown of life, which God has promised to those who love him.

Hebrews 10:36
For you have need of endurance, so that when you have done the will of God you may receive what is promised.

James 1:2-4
Count it all joy, my brothers, when you meet trials of various kinds, for you know that the testing of your faith produces steadfastness. And let steadfastness have its full effect, that you may be perfect and complete, lacking in nothing.

Colossians 1:11
May you be strengthened with all power, according to his glorious might, for all endurance and patience with joy,

1 Corinthians 10:13
No temptation has overtaken you that is not common to man. God is faithful, and he will not let you be tempted beyond your ability, but with the temptation he will also provide the way of escape, that you may be able to endure it.

Hebrews 12:1-3
Therefore, since we are surrounded by so great a cloud of witnesses, let us also lay aside every weight, and sin which clings so closely, and let us run with endurance the race that is set before us, looking to Jesus, the founder and perfecter of our faith, who for the joy that was set before him endured the cross, despising the shame, and is seated at the right hand of the throne of God.

Romans 15:4
For whatever was written in former days was written for our instruction, that through endurance and through the encouragement of the Scriptures we might have hope.

Hebrews 12:7
It is for discipline that you have to endure. God is treating you as sons. For what son is there whom his father does not discipline?

John 16:33
I have said these things to you, that in me you may have peace. In the world you will have tribulation. But take heart; I have overcome the world."

Romans 15:5
May the God of endurance and encouragement grant you to live in such harmony with one another, in accord with Christ Jesus,

Endurance is one of the most difficult disciplines, but it is to the one who endures that the final victory comes.
- Gautama Buddha

Don't pray for a an easy life. Pray for the strength to endure a difficult one."
- Bruce Lee

Commitment [kəˈmitmənt]

the state or quality of being dedicated to a cause or activity

When you get married, you are making a commitment to your spouse. When you sign a letter of intent, you are making a commitment to a college. When you sign your mortgage, you are making a commitment to the bank. When you sign up for a sport, you are making a commitment to your coaches and your teammates. But, what does commitment really mean? The definition of commitment is the quality of being dedicated to a cause or activity. However, a true commitment is much more than that. A commitment is a serious, long-term promise that you make and keep with yourself and others to fully dedicate yourself to and invest the necessary effort to make it happen even when times are tough or you face opposition. A commitment is always followed by an action to fulfill the commitment. If you say you are committed to being a state champion, but you do not do anything to try to achieve that goal, then you were never really committed to it. If action does not occur, then you are only interested in it and not committed to it. What are you doing with your time? Where are you spending your time? Who are you spending that time with? Your answer to those questions will likely tell you the level of your commitment. If you are truly committed to your goals, then you will work on your skills, focus on the things that are important, be at the places that will help you grow, and surround yourself with people that will help you achieve your goals.

Whether you are making an athletic commitment towards a goal, a commitment to your spouse, or a commitment to God, a commitment is your agreement to act. Your commitment is the starting point to achieving your goal. You are making and keeping a promise or pledge to yourself and others to see it through. It is your full investment of yourself, physically, mentally and emotionally to fulfill this promise. It is going all-in and jumping in with both feet. It is your willingness to make individual sacrifices in order to meet your commitment. It is a binding and long-term obligation to continue to work and see the commitment through to completion. It is your pact that you will persevere and overcome whatever obstacles are in your way in order to fulfill the commitment you made. Lastly, it is your agreement to act by aligning your actions with your words. Take your commitments seriously and let your word be your bond.

You will make many commitments in various aspects of your life including to your spouse, your kids, your employers, the church, your health, your hobbies and more. The Bible teaches you that your chief commitment should be to God Himself. You are to be committed to loving God and His ways. Jesus said, "You shall love the Lord your God with all your heart and with all your soul and with all your mind. This is the great and first commandment." Jesus is telling you that every fiber of your being, every facet of your life must be committed to loving and serving God. If you honor that commitment, then you can fulfill your other commitments but you must love God first. To commit to God, you must entrust yourself entirely to Him and entrust your work and activities to God so that they may bear fruit according to His will. Total commitment to God means that Jesus is your sole authority and your guiding light. Being committed to Christ means trusting Him with your life, being fruitful with your works and being a servant to others. That is the commitment you are making when you believe and follow Jesus. Take your commitments seriously. It may not be easy, but it will be worth it.

Reflection: How am I doing with fulfilling the commitments I have made? What about my commitment to God as a believer?

Prayer: Lord, please give me the strength to fulfill my commitments and persevere. Help me to overcome the obstacles in my path so that I can honor my commitments. Show me how to prioritize my life so that I can fulfill my commitments. Amen.

COMMITMENT
IS FINISHING WHAT YOU STARTED EVEN WHEN YOU DON'T FEEL LIKE DOING IT ANYMORE.

"COMMITMENT IS WHAT TRANSFORMS A PROMISE INTO REALITY."

ABRAHAM LINCOLN

DECIDE.
COMMIT.
SUCCEED.

"There is but one degree of commitment; TOTAL."
- Arnie Sherr

"Commitment leads to action.

Action brings your dream closer."
- Marcia Wieder

Commitment [kəˈmitmənt]

the state or quality of being dedicated to a cause or activity

1 Peter 4:19
So then, those who suffer according to God's will should commit themselves to their faithful Creator and continue to do good.

Proverbs 16:3
Commit to the Lord whatever you do, and he will establish your plans.

Luke 9:23-24
Then he said to them all: "Whoever wants to be my disciple must deny themselves and take up their cross daily and follow me. For whoever wants to save their life will lose it, but whoever loses their life for me will save it.

Galatians 2:20
I have been crucified with Christ and I no longer live, but Christ lives in me. The life I now live in the body, I live by faith in the Son of God, who loved me and gave himself for me.

Matthew 5:37
All you need to say is simply 'Yes' or 'No'; anything beyond this comes from the evil one

Proverbs 3:5-6
Trust in the Lord with all your heart and lean not on your own understanding; in all your ways submit to him, and he will make your paths straight

Matthew 22:37
Jesus replied: "'Love the Lord your God with all your heart and with all your soul and with all your mind.

Luke 23:46
Jesus called out with a loud voice, "Father, into your hands I commit my spirit." When he had said this, he breathed his last.

Deuteronomy 27:10
Obey the Lord your God and follow his commands and decrees that I give you today.

1 Kings 8:61
And may your hearts be fully committed to the Lord our God, to live by his decrees and obey his commands, as at this time."

Acts 2:42
They devoted themselves to the apostles' teaching and to fellowship, to the breaking of bread and to prayer.

2 Chronicles 19:9
He gave them these orders: "You must serve faithfully and wholeheartedly in the fear of the Lord.

Deuteronomy 6:5
Love the Lord your God with all your heart and with all your soul and with all your strength.

Toughness [tuhf nis]

strong and durable; not easily broken; capable of great endurance; sturdy; unyielding; to endure hardship or adversity.

"Are you hurt or are you injured?". "Just rub some dirt on it". "Get up, you are fine". "When the going gets tough, the tough get going". You have all experienced your share of "Get Tough" quotes growing up. But what is "toughness"? Toughness is being not easily broken, sturdy, unyielding, strong, resilient and durable. It means you are able to block out the physical pain and mental doubts and still be able to perform at the highest levels even under difficult circumstances. Toughness is exactly what you need on the wrestling mat to achieve the highest level of success. In wrestling, there is a high probability that you will be hurt, that you will experience pain, that you will get beat and that you will face trials and adversity. It may come in the form of a bloody nose, a bruised muscle, extreme fatigue, a loss of a match or even a broken bone. Wrestling is a contact sport. It is a fight and it is hard. Toughness is that small voice in your head that says "Don't Quit. Keep Going. Get up. You Can Do It". You must have toughness both physically and mentally in order to reach the next level of wrestling.

So, how do you get "tough"? I would argue that you have to get out of your comfort zone and push your limits. You need to be willing to fail and be uncomfortable. You have to prepare yourself mentally and program your mind to be an overcomer and remain positive in the face of adversity. You need to be able to continually push yourself to your breaking point and keep going. Being tough, has more to do with the mind than the body. It is a mental fortitude and the conviction to not quit and not give up. It is keeping your poise and composure despite your circumstances. It is your belief and confidence in your abilities and a determination to succeed. Mental toughness is the ability to accept and cope with anxiety in competition and the pressure of the situation. It is the ability to focus on the task at hand in the face of distractions or competition. It is the ability to bounce back from performance setbacks with more resolve and more desire to succeed. It is finding a way to control any negative self-talk and turning it into a positive and actionable task. Mental toughness is learned and it is a key psychological characteristic of any elite athlete.

While the word toughness is not directly mentioned in the Bible, its attributes and characteristics are. The Bible talks about toughness in the form of strength, resiliency, perseverance, and being unbreakable and an overcomer. True toughness is a believer who never stops trusting in God even when things don't go their way. Toughness is going through the storms of life and still praising and serving the Lord. It is recognizing that God will never give up on you and that He died for your salvation. Toughness is standing up for Him and doing what is right in the face of temptation. Toughness is following God's lead and being obedient to His will. Life and sports requires mental toughness when tough times hit. Adversity often reveals your character flaws and reveals your weaknesses. You need to recognize and acknowledge these moments because in 2 Corinthians 12:10 it says, "that when I am weak, then I am strong." Demonstrating real toughness is showing a reliance on God's strength to get you through any trials and trusting Him with the outcome. The mental toughness you should want to see in yourself is less about yourself and more about God. The toughness you seek is revealed in God's character. God has not given up on you and He will never stop pursuing and loving you. No matter what trials you face, God is bigger, stronger and tougher than your circumstances and He will always have your back.

Reflection: How tough am I? Am I relying on God and His strength or on my own stength? Where are areas of my life that I need to get tougher for the Lord?

Prayer: Lord, in my weakness, You are strong. Give me the toughness and the strength to trust You with my circumstances. Thank You for Your grace. Amen

Toughness [tuhf nis]

strong and durable; not easily broken; capable of great endurance; sturdy; unyielding; to endure hardship or adversity.

2 Corinthians 4:7-10
But we have this treasure in jars of clay to show that this all-surpassing power is from God and not from us. We are hard pressed on every side, but not crushed; perplexed, but not in despair; persecuted, but not abandoned; struck down, but not destroyed. We always carry around in our body the death of Jesus, so that the life of Jesus may also be revealed in our body.

Ephesians 6:10-14
Finally, be strong in the Lord and in his mighty power. Put on the full armor of God, so that you can take your stand against the devil's schemes. For our struggle is not against flesh and blood, but against the rulers, against the authorities, against the powers of this dark world and against the spiritual forces of evil in the heavenly realms. Therefore put on the full armor of God, so that when the day of evil comes, you may be able to stand your ground, and after you have done everything, to stand firm.

Joshua 1:9
Have I not commanded you? Be strong and courageous. Do not be afraid; do not be discouraged, for the Lord your God will be with you wherever you go."

2 Corinthians 12:10
That is why, for Christ's sake, I delight in weaknesses, in insults, in hardships, in persecutions, in difficulties. For when I am weak, then I am strong.

Hebrews 6:19
We have this hope as an anchor for the soul, firm and secure. It enters the inner sanctuary behind the curtain,

Psalm 23:4
Even though I walk through the darkest valley, I will fear no evil, for you are with me; your rod and your staff, they comfort me.

2 Corinthians 4:8-9
We are hard pressed on every side, but not crushed; perplexed, but not in despair; persecuted, but not abandoned; struck down, but not destroyed.

Job 17:9
Nevertheless, the righteous will hold to their ways, and those with clean hands will grow stronger.

Hebrews 12:2-3
fixing our eyes on Jesus, the pioneer and perfecter of faith. For the joy set before him he endured the cross, scorning its shame, and sat down at the right hand of the throne of God. Consider him who endured such opposition from sinners, so that you will not grow weary and lose heart.

Psalm 62:6
Truly he is my rock and my salvation; he is my fortress, I will not be shaken.

IT AIN'T ABOUT **HOW HARD** YA HIT.

IT'S ABOUT HOW HARD YOU CAN **GET HIT** AND KEEP MOVING FORWARD.

HOW MUCH YOU CAN TAKE AND KEEP MOVING FORWARD.

THAT'S HOW WINNING IS DONE!

- ROCKY BALBOA

"TOUGHNESS IS IN THE SOUL AND SPIRIT, NOT IN MUSCLES."

ALEX KARRAS

"CONCENTRATION AND MENTAL TOUGHNESS ARE THE MARGINS OF VICTORY."

- BILL RUSSELL

Accountable [uh-koun-tuh-buh l]

subject to the obligation to report, explain, or justify something; responsible; answerable.

Developing athletes who are accountable to themselves and their team is a huge factor to creating a championship culture. It is difficult to display leadership qualities and good teamwork without accountability among the athletes. Accountability is when an athlete takes responsibility for their actions. Many times, when you fail, you blame others for your failures. Accountability is recognizing your own weaknesses and your own shortcomings and taking responsibility for them. It is about understanding your role on the team and doing your part. You are accountable to yourself, your coaches and your teammates. Accountable athletes are trustworthy, dependable and people that take initiative and solve problems. If you are accountable then you show up on time for practices and games, you give your best effort to fulfill your role on the team and obey the team rules. It is about making decisions and being accountable for the consequences of those decisions. Without accountability, teamwork breaks down. The failure of one team member can lead to the failure of the entire team.

How do you show accountability? It starts with having a vision and knowing the rules and expectations. It is always your choice if you do not want to follow the rules. However, being accountable is understanding that you also have to deal with the consequences of your decisions. Accountability is also about honesty. You have to be able to be honest with yourself and your teammates. It is about being honest with yourself and your areas of weakness that you need to work on. It is about taking responsibility when you mess up or fall down instead of blaming others. In order to be accountable, you also need to be able to accept criticism. This is difficult for anyone but it is essential in order to reach your goals. Constructive criticism is important because it allows someone to expose areas of weakness that you may not see yourself. Accept the criticism so that you can be coachable and improve on your skills. Instead of focusing on distractions or things that are out of your control like the referees, your opponent or the coaches, focus on the things that you can control and improve upon.

In life, as on a team, you are called to be accountable. Husbands and wives are accountable to be faithful to each other. Children are accountable to obey their parents. Employees are accountable to their employers to do their job. Students are accountable to their teachers to show up to class. If you choose to not fulfill your responsibilities then there are consequences for your actions. You may get a divorce, you may be grounded, you may be fired or you may fail your class. Disobedience always leads to consequences. Ultimately, you are to be accountable to God in the same way. God calls you to be obedient not because He is a mean God who rules with an iron fist, but because He loves you and wants the best for you. God allows consequences of your sin so that you may turn away from it and turn back to Him. Parents show love to their children in the same way by disciplining their children when that child breaks the rules. Good parents discipline out of love in order to protect their child. It is your choice to sin. But, when you choose to sin, there are always consequences for your actions. Accountability helps you stay on the right path and live a Godly life that is honoring to God and a good witness to others. Be responsible and be accountable to yourself and those around you.

Reflection: Am I taking responsibility for my own decisions and actions or am I blaming others for my failures? Am I able to be honest with myself and see where I am falling short? Am I able to receive criticism without becoming angry or offended?

Prayer: Lord, help me to have the courage and strength to take accountability for my actions. Help me to accept the consequences of my decision and turn to You and Your ways. Thank You for Your guidance and counsel in my life. Amen

Accountable [uh-koun-tuh-buh l]

subject to the obligation to report, explain, or justify something; responsible; answerable.

Proverbs 27:17
As iron sharpens iron, so one person sharpens another.

Hebrews 13:17
Have confidence in your leaders and submit to their authority, because they keep watch over you as those who must give an account. Do this so that their work will be a joy, not a burden, for that would be of no benefit to you.

Romans 14:12
So then, each of us will give an account of ourselves to God.

Galatians 6:1-2
Brothers and sisters, if someone is caught in a sin, you who live by the Spirit should restore that person gently. But watch yourselves, or you also may be tempted. Carry each other's burdens, and in this way you will fulfill the law of Christ.

1 Thessalonians 5:11
Therefore encourage one another and build each other up, just as in fact you are doing.

James 5:16
Therefore confess your sins to each other and pray for each other so that you may be healed. The prayer of a righteous person is powerful and effective.

Ecclesiastes 4:9-12
Two are better than one, because they have a good return for their labor: If either of them falls down, one can help the other up. But pity anyone who falls and has no one to help them up. Also, if two lie down together, they will keep warm. But how can one keep warm alone? Though one may be overpowered, two can defend themselves. A cord of three strands is not quickly broken.

Luke 17:3
So watch yourselves. "If your brother or sister sins against you, rebuke them; and if they repent, forgive them.

Proverbs 15:22
Plans fail for lack of counsel, but with many advisers they succeed.

Matthew 5:37
All you need to say is simply 'Yes' or 'No'; anything beyond this comes from the evil one.

James 5:12
Above all, my brothers and sisters, do not swear—not by heaven or by earth or by anything else. All you need to say is a simple "Yes" or "No." Otherwise you will be condemned.

Matthew 12:36
But I tell you that everyone will have to give account on the day of judgment for every empty word they have spoken.

ACCOUNTABILITY

IS THE GLUE THAT TIES

COMMITMENT

TO RESULTS

PERSONAL ACCOUNTABILITY REQUIRES MINDFULNESS, ACCEPTANCE, HONESTY, AND COURAGE.

- SHELBY MARTIN

Trust [truhst]

Reliance on the integrity, strength, ability, surety, etc., of a person or thing; confidence in the certainty of future payment for property or goods received; credit

A successful team consists of athletes that trust their coaches, trust their teammates and trust the system they are playing in. In order to change the culture of a team, a coach needs to get the athletes to "buy-in" to the vision and processes they have set up to achieve the goals of the team and individuals. The only way that can happen is if there is trust. Trust is putting your reliance, confidence and faith in something or someone. If you trust someone, that means that you think they are reliable, and that you have confidence in them and feel safe with them physically and emotionally. You can't be a good teammate or an elite athlete without trust. No elite athlete in the world has ever competed at the highest level without first being taught the sport by someone else. They had to trust a coach to teach them. To be taught or coached, you have to trust the one coaching you that they know what they are doing and that they have your best interests in mind. You have to trust your teammates to give their best efforts and to compete fairly and safely in the practice room. Each member of the team must establish trust, cultivate trust through their actions and words, and then work to maintain that trust. Each member also needs to be able to trust his team members to make a commitment to the team, its goals and to work competently towards achieving those goals. Trust is essential to learning, growing and reaching your full potential as an athlete and team. The level of trust among the team can set up a culture of success or a culture of failure.

Trust is often times earned over time and based on experience. Trust is difficult because it can be lost as quickly as it is gained. Trusting is uncomfortable because it requires you to be vulnerable and rely on someone or something outside of your control. Trusting is a choice. Many people struggle with trust because they have been burned so many times and let down. However, trust is an important part of life. A life without trust is one consumed with paranoia, fear and doubt. It is true that if you trust someone or something then you run the risk of being let down and hurt. But, if you make the choice to not trust in anything or anyone, then you are also risking the opportunity to experience real growth, love and relationships. You can't have a real relationship without trust. You can't be a good employer or employee without trust. You can't experience God without trust.

God wants you to put your faith and trust in Him. God calls you to believe in Him, His promises and trust Him with your life. Trust leads to belief and belief breeds faith. Faith is placing your confidence in something that is unseen or unproven. Hebrews 11:1 says, "Now faith is confidence in what you hope for and assurance about what you do not see." Although you may not see God physically, you can trust him completely. The more times that you step out of your comfort zone and trust God's word and His promises in your life, the more He will be faithful to fulfill those promises. You trust in the Lord because He alone is truly trustworthy. God is the one constant that will not fail you when you choose to trust Him. Your faith and trust in God will help you combat fear and doubts. I challenge you to let go of the things that you are trying to control in your life and trust God with them. Let Him take control, trust Him and He will be faithful.

Reflection: Am I living in fear or am I trusting God with my life? Are there areas of my life that I am not giving up control to God?

Prayer: Lord, please give me the ability to trust You more with areas of my life. Help me to give up control and allow me to trust You alone. Thank You Lord, Amen.

Trust [truhst]

Reliance on the integrity, strength, ability, surety, etc., of a person or thing; confidence in the certainty of future payment for property or goods received; credit

Isaiah 26:3-4
You will keep in perfect peace those whose minds are steadfast, because they trust in you Trust in the Lord forever, for the Lord, the Lord himself, is the Rock eternal.

Proverbs 3:5-8
Trust in the Lord with all your heart and lean not on your own understanding; in all your ways submit to him, and he will make your paths straight. Do not be wise in your own eyes; fear the Lord and shun evil. This will bring health to your body and nourishment to your bones.

Psalm 56:3-4
When I am afraid, I put my trust in you. In God, whose word I praise—in God I trust and am not afraid. What can mere mortals do to me?

Jeremiah 29:11
For I know the plans I have for you," declares the Lord, "plans to prosper you and not to harm you, plans to give you hope and a future.

Psalm 13:5
But I trust in your unfailing love; my heart rejoices in your salvation.

Mark 11:24
Therefore I tell you, whatever you ask for in prayer, believe that you have received it, and it will be yours.

Psalm 40:4
Blessed is the one who trusts in the Lord, who does not look to the proud, to those who turn aside to false gods.

Philippians 4:6-7
Do not be anxious about anything, but in every situation, by prayer and petition, with thanksgiving, present your requests to God. And the peace of God, which transcends all understanding, will guard your hearts and your minds in Christ Jesus.

Psalm 37:5
Commit your way to the Lord; trust in him and he will do this:

Psalm 31:14-15
But I trust in you, Lord; I say, "You are my God." My times are in your hands; deliver me from the hands of my enemies, from those who pursue me.

Romans 4:20-21
Yet he did not waver through unbelief regarding the promise of God, but was strengthened in his faith and gave glory to God, 21 being fully persuaded that God had power to do what he had promised.

Psalm 9:10
Those who know your name trust in you, for you, Lord, have never forsaken those who seek you.

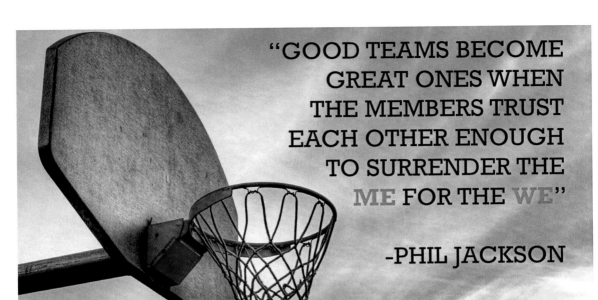

"GOOD TEAMS BECOME GREAT ONES WHEN THE MEMBERS TRUST EACH OTHER ENOUGH TO SURRENDER THE ME FOR THE WE"

-PHIL JACKSON

"Without TRUST we don't truly collaborate; we merely coordinate or, at best, cooperate. It is TRUST that transforms a group of people into a team."
- Stephen M.R. Covey

TRUST YOUR TEAM
TRUST YOUR COACH
TRUST YOURSELF

Dedication [ded-i-key-shuh n]

to devote wholly and earnestly, as to some person or purpose: complete and wholehearted devotion

Thousands of miles driven to and from wrestling practices and tournaments. Hundreds of miles of pounding the pavement on runs or peddling on a stationary bike. Countless hours of drilling takedowns, stand ups and breakdowns. Gallons of sweat and endless piles of dirty laundry. An untold number of missed meals and cotton mouth. A few broken bones and several bloody noses. Wrestling is not easy. Success is not easy. Achieving your goals is not easy. It takes dedication.

A commitment is sticking to your decision to do something. Dedication is your devotion to seeing that commitment through. Wrestling is a sport that requires dedication in order to be successful. It is one thing to have an interest in wrestling, but until you become dedicated to the sport, you will not find the success you are looking for. Dedication is about putting in the time and the effort necessary to achieve your goals. It is working out when you are sick and tired of working out. It is staying disciplined to your diet when you don't feel like it. It is going to bed early when you want to stay up late. Dedication is committing and devoting yourself whole heartedly to achieving your goals. There are no shortcuts to getting where you want to be. It takes practice, time, discipline, effort, learning, responsibility and accountability. All of these things are wrapped up in your dedication to see them through. Once you have chosen a direction and made a decision to act, you must dedicate yourself to your cause. Dedication means your actions align with your aspirations. It is going out and actually doing the things you know are necessary to achieve your goals. It is a 100% commitment and a complete immersion of yourself into your cause or purpose.

The dedication that is required to excel in sports is the same dedication that you are to have with God. God wants you to dedicate or devote yourselves wholly to Him. The priority of your devotion should always be to God first. You are to be 100% committed and devoted to God. As a believer, you are to be dedicated to living a life honoring to God and making much of Him. You are set apart through faith for a special purpose. That purpose is to bring others to know and believe in Jesus. You need only to look to the cross to see God's dedication to you. God showed His devotion and love for you by sending His son, Jesus, to die on the cross so that you can be saved. Now, you are to live your life dedicated to making sure others may know Jesus and experience God's grace as well. God is looking for a 100% commitment and dedication from you. He doesn't want you to be only interested in Him. He is seeking your complete dedication to Him. A life dedicated to God is a life of worship, thanksgiving, dependence, trust and commitment. It is a life dedicated to making much of God and less of yourself. It is a life that is others focused rather than self-focused. Dedication to God is the only way to truly experience God and an authentic life.

Reflection: Am I committed and dedicated to God or am I being lukewarm with my walk? Am I living a life that is dedicated to God? Is God my number one priority and devotion?

Prayer: Lord, help strengthen my dedication and commitment to You. Help me to be fully devoted to worshipping and trusting You. Lord, thank You for demonstrating Your dedication to me through Jesus. Help me to make much of You. Amen.

Achievement is Impossible Without Dedication

Dedication [ded-i-key-shuh n]

to devote wholly and earnestly, as to some person or purpose: complete and wholehearted devotion

Revelation 3:16
So, because you are lukewarm—neither hot nor cold—I am about to spit you out of my mouth.

Romans 12:1-2
Therefore, I urge you, brothers and sisters, in view of God's mercy, to offer your bodies as a living sacrifice, holy and pleasing to God—this is your true and proper worship. Do not conform to the pattern of this world, but be transformed by the renewing of your mind. Then you will be able to test and approve what God's will is—his good, pleasing and perfect will.

1 Corinthians 6:20
you were bought at a price. Therefore honor God with your bodies.

Proverbs 3:9
Honor the Lord with your wealth, with the firstfruits of all your crops;

1 Thessalonians 2:12
encouraging, comforting and urging you to live lives worthy of God, who calls you into his kingdom and glory.

2 Corinthians 5:15
And he died for all, that those who live should no longer live for themselves but for him who died for them and was raised again.

Romans 14:8
If we live, we live for the Lord; and if we die, we die for the Lord. So, whether we live or die, we belong to the Lord.

1 Corinthians 10:31
So whether you eat or drink or whatever you do, do it all for the glory of God.

Deuteronomy 6:5
Love the Lord your God with all your heart and with all your soul and with all your strength.

Colossians 3:17
And whatever you do, whether in word or deed, do it all in the name of the Lord Jesus, giving thanks to God the Father through him.

1 Chronicles 26:27
Some of the plunder taken in battle they dedicated for the repair of the temple of the Lord.

Mark 12:30
Love the Lord your God with all your heart and with all your soul and with all your mind and with all your strength.

Jeremiah 29:13
You will seek me and find me when you seek me with all your heart.

DEDICATION AND COMMITMENT ARE WHAT TRANSFER DREAMS INTO REALITIES.

The price of success is hard work, dedication to the job at hand, and the determination that whether we win or lose, we have applied the best of ourselves to the task at hand.

(Vince Lombardi)

IF YOU BELIEVE IN YOURSELF, HAVE DEDICATION AND PRIDE AND NEVER QUIT, YOU'LL BE A WINNER.

Sacrifice [sak-ruh-fahys]

to surrender or give up for the sake of something else considered as having a higher or more pressing claim

If you stood in front of a room full of young high school or college wrestlers and asked them, "Who wants to be a state champion or a national champion in the sport," You would find almost every hand would go up. Knowing what you want to be or do is certainly the first step. However, the difference between actually making it happen will ultimately come down to sacrifice. What are you willing to sacrifice today, tomorrow and every week following in order to achieve that goal? Most times you will find that the sacrifice is too great and kids will quit trying. Why? Because sacrifice is hard. It is not easy to give up things that you like or want to do. Sacrifice requires you to give up the things that you WANT, in order to do the things that you NEED to do. The physical pain is too much. The strain on relationships and time commitments are too high. The discipline and obedience required on your nutrition, sleep and diet are too taxing. These are just a few of the reasons that many athletes never reach their goals. The truth is that you will never reach your full and great potential without sacrifice. Every wrestler has dreams, talents and aspirations to be the best, but few embrace the sacrifice necessary to achieve those dreams. Claiming to want to be a champion is the easy part. Understanding and actually doing what is required to be a champion is the hard part. What you are willing to sacrifice may be the deciding factor on whether or not you achieve your goal. You have to have the passion, will and faith to believe that your sacrifices now will produce greater rewards later. This may require that you suffer short-term losses in order to experience long-term gains. In order to be a champion, it will require that you sacrifice your time, body, mind, social life, comfort level, food, vacations, sleep and much more. It certainly will not be easy, but in my experience, it will be worth it.

The same is true in life. Life will require sacrifices. You will need to sacrifice your time, money and resources for your children, your spouse, your responsibilities or your job. There will be many times that you will not feel like sacrificing your wants or desires, but it is necessary for the well-being and benefit of others. As a believer, your focus is to be outward and for the benefit of others. If you are being honest with yourself, you are probably selfish and self-focused. It is natural. You want to be selfish and you have a "Me" first attitude. But, God calls you to use your talents and your gifts to bring others to Christ and that requires sacrifice.

From the time of Adam and Eve through the time of Jesus Christ, God's people practiced animal sacrifice. They were commanded to offer an animal without blemish as a sacrifice to the Lord as payment for their sin. The sacrificial lamb was used as a reminder to the people of their sin and that the requirement of sin is death. This ordinance was given to remind the people that there was penalty for their sin. Jesus Christ, God's only Son, came into the world and offered Himself as a sacrifice for all people's sin. Jesus came, died and was resurrected so that all people can be saved through His sacrifice. Even though animal sacrifices have ended and are no longer required because Jesus fulfilled the need for sacrifices, God still asks us to sacrifice. God asks you to give to the Lord whatever He requires of your time, your energies and your possessions to further His work. He asks you to love your neighbors and to be living sacrifices that glorify Him with the way you live your life. God wants you to sacrifice your sinful desires and choose obedience and repentance with a humble heart. These sacrifices will glorify God and bring others to know Christ and experience salvation. The rewards for your sacrifice may not be earthly, but they certainly are eternal and far outweigh anything you could gain here on earth. Living a life that glorifies God may not be easy, but it will be worth it...in this life or the next.

Reflection: Am I willing to sacrfice my selfish desires for the sake of others? Am I living a life of sacrifice that is honoring to God?

Prayer: Lord, help me to put others first and make sacrifices that benefit others. Help me to set aside my own wants in order to follow Your will for me. Amen

"TO GIVE ANYTHING LESS THAN YOUR BEST IS TO SACRIFICE THE GIFT."

STEVE PREFONTAINE
LEGENDARY LONG DISTANCE RUNNER

The good and the great are only separated by their willingness to sacrifice

- Kareem Abdul-Jabbar

Sacrifice [sak-ruh-fahys]

to surrender or give up for the sake of something else considered as having a higher or more pressing claim

Romans 12:1-2
Therefore, I urge you, brothers and sisters, in view of God's mercy, to offer your bodies as a living sacrifice, holy and pleasing to God—this is your true and proper worship. 2 Do not conform to the pattern of this world, but be transformed by the renewing of your mind. Then you will be able to test and approve what God's will is—his good, pleasing and perfect will.

John 15:12-14
This is my commandment, that you love one another as I have loved you. Greater love has no one than this, that someone lay down his life for his friends. You are my friends if you do what I command you.

Hebrews 13:16
And do not forget to do good and to share with others, for with such sacrifices God is pleased.

Romans 5:8
But God demonstrates his own love for us in this: While we were still sinners, Christ died for us.

John 3:16
For God so loved the world that he gave his one and only Son, that whoever believes in him shall not perish but have eternal life.

Philippians 2:4
not looking to your own interests but each of you to the interests of the others.

Psalm 51:16-17
You do not delight in sacrifice, or I would bring it; you do not take pleasure in burnt offerings. My sacrifice, O God, is a broken spirit; a broken and contrite heart you, God, will not despise.

Hebrews 13:15
Through Jesus, therefore, let us continually offer to God a sacrifice of praise—the fruit of lips that openly profess his name.

1 Samuel 15:22
But Samuel replied: "Does the Lord delight in burnt offerings and sacrifices as much as in obeying the Lord? To obey is better than sacrifice, and to heed is better than the fat of rams.

Hosea 6:6
For I desire mercy, not sacrifice, and acknowledgment of God rather than burnt offerings.

Leviticus 17:11
For the life of a creature is in the blood, and I have given it to you to make atonement for yourselves on the altar; it is the blood that makes atonement for one's life.

You have to fight to reach your dream. You have to sacrifice and work hard for it. - Lionel Messi

Peace [pees]

untroubled; tranquil; content. a state of tranquillity or serenity:

One of the biggest struggles I had as a wrestler throughout my high school and college career was how to mentally prepare for a match. I would find myself getting too psyched up or investing too much emotion into an upcoming match. This caused me to experience increased anxiety and nervousness before I took the mat. It also caused me to warm-up my body too early to the point that I was tired before I even walked out on the mat. I have also learned that I do not perform well when I am angry or overly anxious. These emotions clouded my judgment, placed doubt in my mind and caused my body to be tight or try too hard. When your emotions are heightened it causes your body to go into a "fight or flight" mode and your mind falls into a state of flux and becomes full of racing thoughts. This causes you to panic which results in your body expending more energy at a faster rate, increased heart rate, increased respiration and muscle tension. The result is that your body will fatigue much faster and you will not be able to perform at your peak level. My failure to properly approach the matches with the right mindset caused my performance to suffer. The element I was lacking was peace. When your mind is at peace, you are calm, relaxed, and confident. This mindset allows your body to feel in control and perform at a higher level.

How do you develop peace of mind? For me, it was a change of mindset and approach to my matches. It was looking at each match like I approached practice. It is said that you perform how you practice. I had to train my mind to approach my matches in the same way that I approached practice. For me, it was about going to work. It was punching my time card and focusing on all the little tasks at hand. It was about focusing on the things that I could control like my footwork, scoring points, continuing to move forward, working for the pin, controlling the tie-ups, and staying offensive. I had to stop getting caught up in the idea of winning or losing and I stop worrying about who my opponent was or who he had beaten before. All of those things were out of my control. I started looking at my opponents as if they had no names or no faces. They were merely objects in my way to achieving my goal. I only focused on the things that I could control. The things like how I trained, my conditioning, my techniques and my mindset. Peace for me was trying to keep everything in proper perspective. Win or lose, I was going to give my best effort and leave it all out on the mat. Peace is walking off the mat whether you won or you lost with no regrets. If I trained hard and gave my best effort and never gave up, then I was going to be okay with the outcome of the match, win or lose. I still disliked losing, but I could have peace knowing that I laid it all out on the mat but came up short that day. Peace is the ability to change the things that are within your control, accept the things that are out of your control, and having the wisdom to know the difference. Peace is knowing that it is just a sport and does not define who you are as a person.

In life, you will face trials. Some trials will be in your control and some will be beyond your control. The important thing is to understand that God is ultimately in control. It is your trust and faith in Him alone that can give you true peace and contentment. It is important to keep things in proper perspective and realize what truly is important in life. Don't sweat the small stuff, be thankful and trust that God is in control. Put your faith in Him and His peace will be with you always.

Reflection: Am I allowing worry and fear control my life? Am I placing my trust and faith in God that He is in control of my circumstances?

Prayer: Lord, thank You that You are in control. Help me to trust You and accept the things that I can not control. Give me peace that You are guiding my steps and my life. Amen.

Peace [pees]

untroubled; tranquil; content. a state of tranquillity or serenity:

2 Thessalonians 3:16
Now may the Lord of peace himself give you peace at all times and in every way. The Lord be with all of you.

Philippians 4:6
Do not be anxious about anything, but in every situation, by prayer and petition, with thanksgiving, present your requests to God.

John 16:33
"I have told you these things, so that in me you may have peace. In this world you will have trouble. But take heart! I have overcome the world."

Isaiah 26:3
You will keep in perfect peace those whose minds are steadfast, because they trust in you.

1 Peter 5:6-7
Humble yourselves, therefore, under the mighty hand of God so that at the proper time he may exalt you, casting all your anxieties on him, because he cares for you.

Romans 12:18
If it is possible, as far as it depends on you, live at peace with everyone.

1 Peter 3:11
They must turn from evil and do good; they must seek peace and pursue it.

Romans 15:13
May the God of hope fill you with all joy and peace as you trust in him, so that you may overflow with hope by the power of the Holy Spirit.

Proverbs 12:20
Deceit is in the hearts of those who plot evil, but those who promote peace have joy.

Galatians 5:22
But the fruit of the Spirit is love, joy, peace, forbearance, kindness, goodness, faithfulness,

Romans 14:19
Let us therefore make every effort to do what leads to peace and to mutual edification.

Isaiah 12:2
Surely God is my salvation; I will trust and not be afraid. The Lord, the Lord himself, is my strength and my defense; he has become my salvation."

Colossians 3:15
Let the peace of Christ rule in your hearts, since as members of one body you were called to peace. And be thankful.

Philippians 4:7
And the peace of God, which transcends all understanding, will guard your hearts and your minds in Christ Jesus.

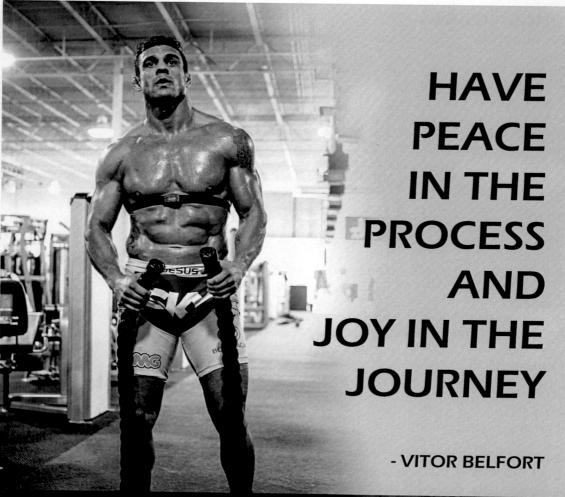

HAVE PEACE IN THE PROCESS AND JOY IN THE JOURNEY

- VITOR BELFORT

SUCCESS IS PEACE OF MIND, WHICH IS A DIRECT RESULT OF SELF-SATISFACTION IN KNOWING YOU MADE THE EFFORT TO BECOME THE BEST OF WHICH YOU ARE CAPABLE.

- JOHN WOODEN

Confidence [kon-fi-duh ns]

having strong belief or full assurance; sure of oneself; having no uncertainty about one's own abilities; full trust.

Henry Ford once said, "Whether you think you can or you think you can't, you're right." So much of your success as an athlete depends on your confidence. Your confidence is how strongly you believe in your ability to achieve your goals. You may have all of the skills and ability in the world to be a great wrestler, but if you don't believe you have that ability, then you will not perform up to your potential. Confidence demonstrates faith in your abilities and your preparation. It keeps you positive, motivated, intense, focused, poised and emotionally in control. You will hear coaches all the time yelling, "Be confident. Take a shot" or "Believe in yourself. You can do it". This is all about trusting your skills, your training and everything that has prepared you for that match and believe that you are capable of achieving your goal. Out on the mat, there is no room for self-doubt and hesitation. You cannot have negative self-talk or walk out on that mat with a fear of failure and truly be successful. Confidence is the key to reaching your potential.

How do you develop confidence? Confidence is not an emotion, you can't feel it. Confidence is a belief, which makes it a thought. Feelings can change based on your circumstances or mood, but a belief has lasting power and stands on its own despite your circumstances. There will be many times when you are losing or things are not going your way that you will not "feel" very confident. But, confidence is "knowing" that you are capable of scoring and continue to press forward and keep battling. Confidence is a skill, it can be learned. Confidence is learned through experience, focus, effort, repetition and small victories. It is said that "Success breeds success". That is because when you have success, you increase your confidence and you are willing to go a little bit further each time you try. The greatest disruption to confidence is failure. Failure can lead to negative self-talk, anxiety and doubt. The secret to maintaining confidence is to approach failure with a proper perspective. Failure can be your greatest teacher and can motivate you to bigger and better things. Failure is necessary in order to push your limits. Do not fear failure, learn to embrace it, learn from it and let it motivate you. People with confidence approach difficult tasks as challenges to be mastered rather than threats to be avoided. Control the things that you can control and continue to focus on improving your skills, maximizing your efforts and the victories will take care of themselves. Your level of confidence may be the single most important mental key to your success.

The Bible speaks about how it is important for you to live out your life confidently trusting in the Lord and living in an effective way to make much of Him. You are to be confident in God. You can have full assurance in His promises and His truths. Again, this confidence is not a feeling, it is a belief. Every day of your life you have a choice. You can either focus on the obstacles and circumstances before you, or you can be confident and trust that God is in control and He is pouring His strength into you to be able to persevere and overcome your circumstances. Your confidence, or lack of confidence, directly affects how you approach everything in life. In 2 Timothy 1:7 it says, "For God has not given you a spirit of fear and timidity, but of power, love, and self-discipline." Be confident in the Lord, trust in Him. In Philippians 1:6, it says, "For I am confident of this very thing, that He who began a good work in you will perfect it until the day of Christ Jesus." You are called to be confident in yourselves and most importantly be confident in the Lord in all ways and for all things.

Reflection: Do I have confidence in myself? Do I have confidence in God?

Prayer: Lord, thank You for Your promises. Thank You that You are in control. Help me to have confidence in Your truths and trust You with my life. Amen.

Confidence [kon-fi-duh nt]

having strong belief or full assurance; sure of oneself; having no uncertainty about one's own abilities; full trust.

Hebrews 4:16
Let us then approach God's throne of grace with confidence, so that we may receive mercy and find grace to help us in our time of need.

Philippians 1:6
being confident of this, that he who began a good work in you will carry it on to completion until the day of Christ Jesus.

Proverbs 3:26
for the Lord will be at your side and will keep your foot from being snared.

1 John 5:14
This is the confidence we have in approaching God: that if we ask anything according to his will, he hears us.

Philippians 4:13
I can do all this through him who gives me strength.

Hebrews 13:5-6
Keep your lives free from the love of money and be content with what you have, because God has said, "Never will I leave you; never will I forsake you." So we say with confidence, "The Lord is my helper; I will not be afraid. What can mere mortals do to me?"

Isaiah 41:10
So do not fear, for I am with you; do not be dismayed, for I am your God. I will strengthen you and help you; I will uphold you with my righteous right hand.

Philippians 4:6-7
Do not be anxious about anything, but in every situation, by prayer and petition, with thanksgiving, present your requests to God. 7 And the peace of God, which transcends all understanding, will guard your hearts and your minds in Christ Jesus.

Deuteronomy 31:6
Be strong and courageous. Do not be afraid or terrified because of them, for the Lord your God goes with you; he will never leave you nor forsake you."

Proverbs 3:5-6
Trust in the Lord with all your heart and lean not on your own understanding;
in all your ways submit to him, and he will make your paths straight.

Acts 1:8
But you will receive power when the Holy Spirit comes on you; and you will be my witnesses in Jerusalem, and in all Judea and Samaria, and to the ends of the earth."

Joshua 1:9
Have I not commanded you? Be strong and courageous. Do not be afraid; do not be discouraged, for the Lord your God will be with you wherever you go."

CONFIDENCE is not
a guarantee of success, but
a pattern of thinking that will improve
your likelihood of success,
a tenacious search for ways to make
things work.

John Eliot

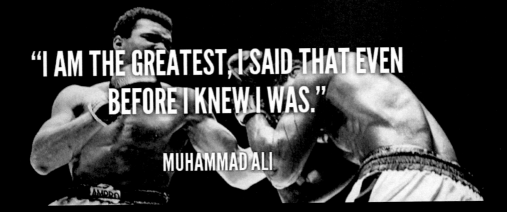

"I AM THE GREATEST, I SAID THAT EVEN BEFORE I KNEW I WAS."

MUHAMMAD ALI

TO BE A GREAT CHAMPION YOU MUST BELIEVE YOU ARE THE BEST. IF YOU'RE NOT, PRETEND YOU ARE."

-MUHAMMAD ALI

"MY CONFIDENCE COMES FROM THE DAILY GRIND. TRAINING MY BUTT OFF DAY IN AND DAY OUT."
-HOPE SOLO

INHALE CONFIDENCE. EXHALE DOUBT.

Competitive [kuh m-pet-i-tiv]

having a strong desire to compete or to succeed.to strive to outdo another; engage in a contest

I have to be honest, I do not like to lose. It does not matter what game I am playing, I want to win. I truly enjoy competing. It may be the challenge of the game or my desire to be the best I can be in whatever I am doing that drives me. I am not sure, but I know I have a strong competitive spirit. Being competitive for me is more about pursuing excellence and challenging myself than beating an opponent. Competition helps expose my strengths and weaknesses, pushes me to improve and gives me benchmarks to strive for. I find competition to be a motivator and a driving force to self-improvement. When I was wrestling, I always wanted to practice with a guy in the room that was bigger and stronger than me. That is how I believed I got better. I wanted to be challenged and pushed. You do not improve by cutting corners and taking the easy way out. You have to push yourself and be willing to fail in order to truly succeed. Being competitive is about seeking excellence by being your best. It is about being better tomorrow than you were yesterday. Each and every day you have to work to be a better version of yourself.

The key to being competitive is to keep competition in a proper perspective. John Wooden once said, "Sports do not build character. They reveal it." Sports is competition and competition can bring out the best and the worst in people. Competition is a part of life. You will compete in sports, in school for grades, in the workplace for a job and virtually everywhere else in this world for what you want. You will find that everything in life that you really want will not just be handed to you. You will need to earn it. The problem with competition is that it can also have negative effects. The problem is your motivation. If your motivation is selfishness or attention and glory for yourself then competition may reveal poor character. Competition can bring out jealousy, deceit, envy, depression, conceit and cause broken relationships. It is important that you have an attitude of humility in victory and defeat. To show concern and care for the welfare of others. That the way you compete matters more than the outcome of the competition. That you play fair, be respectful and be humble at all times. You must compete in a way that reflects honor to God in the eyes of those who see you and participate in the competition with you. That the goal of competition is the pursuit of excellence and not the pursuit of self-aggrandizement. Ultimately, that pursuit of excellence is pursuing and doing the best you can with the gifts and abilities God has given to you for the glory of God. Winning may create a platform for you to reach others for God's glory and give back to others. Remember that all of your talents and gifts come from God. Whatever you do, you are to do for His glory and to make much of Him. Let your competitive nature strive for the things of excellence. The things that cause the name of Jesus to be honored and cause people to recognize their sin, repent, and live a life that glorifies God. As a believer, you must learn to turn your innate spirit of competitiveness toward good use and strive for excellence and the eternal prize. It is imperative that you keep your focus on the Audience of One, Jesus Christ.

"I have fought the good fight, I have finished the race, I have kept the faith." - 2 Timothy 4:7

Reflection: Am I keeping competition in its proper perspective? Am I honoring God with my attitude and actions during competition? Am I seeking my own glory or glory for God?

Prayer: Lord, thank You for my talents and abilities. I pray that I can use the gifts that You have given me to honor and glorify You. Help me to stay humble and thankful in all that I do. I pray that You will use any success I have achieved through Your blessings to further Your kingdom and reach others for You. Amen

Competitive [kuh m-pet-i-tiv]

having a strong desire to compete or to succeed.to strive to outdo another; engage in a contest

1 Corinthians 9:24-25
Do you not know that in a race all the runners run, but only one gets the prize? Run in such a way as to get the prize. Everyone who competes in the games goes into strict training. They do it to get a crown that will not last, but we do it to get a crown that will last forever.

Philippians 3:14
I press on toward the goal to win the prize for which God has called me heavenward in Christ Jesus.

Philippians 2:3-4
Do nothing out of selfish ambition or vain conceit. Rather, in humility value others above yourselves, not looking to your own interests but each of you to the interests of the others.

2 Timothy 2:5
Similarly, anyone who competes as an athlete does not receive the victor's crown except by competing according to the rules.

Colossians 3:23-24
Whatever you do, work at it with all your heart, as working for the Lord, not for human masters, since you know that you will receive an inheritance from the Lord as a reward. It is the Lord Christ you are serving.

Galatians 2:20
I have been crucified with Christ and I no longer live, but Christ lives in me. The life I now live in the body, I live by faith in the Son of God, who loved me and gave himself for me.

Matthew 5:16
In the same way, let your light shine before others, that they may see your good deeds and glorify your Father in heaven.

Colossians 3:17
And whatever you do, whether in word or deed, do it all in the name of the Lord Jesus, giving thanks to God the Father through him.

2 Corinthians 8:7
But since you excel in everything—in faith, in speech, in knowledge, in complete earnestness and in the love we have kindled in you[a]—see that you also excel in this grace of giving.

Titus 2:7
In everything set them an example by doing what is good. In your teaching show integrity, seriousness

Galatians 6:4
Each one should test their own actions. Then they can take pride in themselves alone, without comparing themselves to someone else,

1 Corinthians 10:31
So whether you eat or drink or whatever you do, do it all for the glory of God.

Proverbs 16:3
Commit to the Lord whatever you do and he will establish your plans.

The healthiest competition
occurs when average people win
by putting above average effort.

Colin Powell

"THE ULTIMATE VICTORY IN COMPETITION IS DERIVED FROM THE INNER SATISFACTION OF KNOWING THAT YOU HAVE DONE YOUR BEST AND THAT YOU HAVE GOTTEN THE MOST OUT OF WHAT YOU HAD TO GIVE."

- HOWARD COSELL

LOOK IN THE
MIRROR...
THAT'S YOUR
COMPETITION.

Competition is a good thing; it forces us to do our BEST.

- Nancy Pearcey

Hope [hohp]

the feeling that what is wanted can be had or that events will turn out for the best: to look forward to with desire and reasonable confidence.

Why do you train? Why do you compete? Why do you push yourself to get better? What if you knew that no matter what you did and no matter how hard you trained, that you would never reach your goals? That you would not win, would not succeed and that failure was imminent no matter if you gave your best efforts? Would that negatively affect your training, your attitude and your motivation? I imagine that you would likely experience anxiety, frustration, anger, lack of motivation, helplessness, despair or even depression. Why? Because you would have lost hope. Hope is the key to success. Hope is believing that something good may happen. Hope allows you to persevere, to be motivated and to believe that you can accomplish whatever you put your mind to. You train because you believe it will pay off and that you can win. Hope gives you the ability to stay positive, to keep fighting and to keep pressing on. Hope says that you can do it, you can overcome, and you can keep going because there is light at the end of the tunnel. Hope says try one more time, don't quit, and that it is going to work this time. As athletes, you need hope to achieve your goals.

I have seen heavy underdogs knock off the top seeds at the national tournament year after year. I have seen wrestlers losing by 14 points in the third period come back to pull out a victory. They did not quit trying because they still had hope of a victory. That is why you wrestle the matches until the final whistle and don't rely on the seeding, the rankings, or your opponent's reputation. If you believe that there is no way to win, then there would be no hope. The truth is that anyone can beat anyone on any given day and that there is always hope for a victory. Have faith in your abilities, your coaches, your training and never give up hope. Win or lose you must keep trying.

The same is true in life. Hope is critical to human survival and our emotional well-being. Suffering, pain and despair are all a part of the human experience. Your faith in God allows you to have hope. Hope in God is trusting and having faith that God has your past, present and your future in His control and that He is working it out for His good. You can be confident that your faith in Jesus Christ as your personal Lord and savior will lead to an eternal life with Him. That is the hope that is promised in His word. Life is difficult at times. Hope anchors you to God and gives you peace and the ability to persevere and endure. Without hope there would be despair. Despair can only live where hope has died. Hope is the lifeblood to your spiritual survival and can enable you to overcome the pain and hurt that this life may cause. You need hope. Even a whisper of hope can be enough to keep you pressing on. No situation, no matter how dire or bleak, can defeat you if you don't let it. Trust God and don't give up hope. Jesus entered this world to give you hope. You now have hope for forgiveness, hope for eternity with God, and hope for a new life in Him.

Reflection: Have I lost hope? What is ruling my life? Is it hope or despair? Do I trust God's promises and believe His word? Is my hope truly in the Lord?

Prayer: Lord, thank You for blessings and Jesus. Thank You that I now have a hope that surpasses any pain or suffering I may endure here on earth. Thank You for Your grace and forgiveness. Help me to have hope in You and continue to persevere until You call me home. Thank You for the hope that has eternal value. Amen.

> Everything that is done in the world is done by hope
> - Martin Luther King Jr

Hope [hohp]

the feeling that what is wanted can be had or that events will turn out for the best: to look forward to with desire and reasonable confidence.

Romans 5:2-5
through whom we have gained access by faith into this grace in which we now stand. And we boast in the hope of the glory of God. Not only so, but we also glory in our sufferings, because we know that suffering produces perseverance; perseverance, character; and character, hope. And hope does not put us to shame, because God's love has been poured out into our hearts through the Holy Spirit, who has been given to us.

Romans 15:13
May the God of hope fill you with all joy and peace as you trust in him, so that you may overflow with hope by the power of the Holy Spirit.

Jeremiah 29:11
For I know the plans I have for you," declares the Lord, "plans to prosper you and not to harm you, plans to give you hope and a future.

Job 11:18
You will be secure, because there is hope; you will look about you and take your rest in safety.

Lamentations 3:22-23
Because of the Lord's great love we are not consumed, for his compassions never fail. They are new every morning; great is your faithfulness.

Psalm 43:5
Why, my soul, are you downcast? Why so disturbed within me? Put your hope in God, for I will yet praise him, my Savior and my God

2 Corinthians 4:16
Therefore we do not lose heart. Though outwardly we are wasting away, yet inwardly we are being renewed day by day.

Romans 12:12
Be joyful in hope, patient in affliction, faithful in prayer.

Deuteronomy 31:6
Be strong and courageous. Do not be afraid or terrified because of them, for the Lord your God goes with you; he will never leave you nor forsake you."

Psalm 39:7
"But now, Lord, what do I look for? My hope is in you.

Proverbs 23:18
There is surely a future hope for you, and your hope will not be cut off.

Titus 1:2
in the hope of eternal life, which God, who does not lie, promised before the beginning of time,

AN ATHLETE CANNOT
RUN WITH MONEY IN
HIS POCKETS. HE
MUST RUN WITH
HOPE IN HIS HEART
AND DREAMS IN HIS
HEAD

-EMIL ZATOPEK
3x Gold Medalist 1952

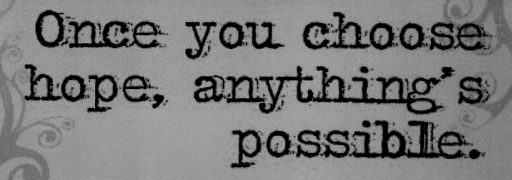

Once you choose
hope, anything's
possible.

– Christopher Reeve

WHEN THE WORLD
SAYS GIVE UP.
HOPE WHISPERS
TRY IT ONE MORE
TIME.

Obedience [oh-bee-dee-uh ns]

the act or practice of obeying; dutiful or submissive compliance:

If you cheat on a test, you could be kicked out of school. If you break the speed limit in your car, you could cause an accident or be fined. If you go skiing in an area where the signs tell you not to, you could end up breaking bones or losing your life. It is said that rules are made to be broken, but in reality, rules are made to ensure safety and guidance. You have a choice to obey or not to obey the rules. Obedience is making a decision to submit to authority and comply with their direction. When it comes to sports, there are rules that should not be broken. Cheating and unsportsmanlike behavior have no place in athletics. Obedience to the rules helps prevent injuries, promotes fair play and encourages good sportsmanship. Unfortunately, many athletes have failed to obey the rules in order to gain an advantage over their opponents. They have taken illegal substances, taken cheap shots or cheated in order to win. That "win at all costs" mentality misses the point of sports. Sports are meant to guide athletes in the development of character, teach life lessons and challenge them to be a better version of themselves. Obeying the rules, your coaches and the officials are an essential part of any sport. When you make the decision to obey, you are surrendering your own preferences, rights or desires for the sake of someone else. Obedience is hard because it often requires doing the exact opposite of what you want to do in order to do what you should do. Obedience is also an expression of trust. When you submit to your coaches instruction you are trusting that they have your best interests in mind. Coaches will ask you to go the extra mile. They will bark orders and instruction to push you to your limits and to stretch you out of your comfort zone. Will you obey or will you question it? Will you grumble or embrace it knowing that it will make you better? Obedience is a key character trait that you need to develop to be successful.

Growing up, my father was a tough disciplinarian. To say obedience was emphasized in my home would be an understatement. However, as I grew older I came to realize that the discipline I received was for my best interest and to protect me from myself. I found the same thing when I was a collegiate wrestler. I did not always see eye to eye with my coach, but I began to trust and obey what he had to say. That obedience led to growth and improvement in my wrestling. When you are young, you think you know everything there is to know. It is not until you look back on life that you realize how little you actually knew. Obedience is not always easy but it is necessary and usually helps keep you safe and leads to growth.

When you obey, you are submitting to someone or something. Many people look at submission as a weakness, but the act of submission can be a sign of strength. Many times it takes more strength to obey than to disobey. In fact, God wants your obedience. Obedience is a test of loyalty and trust. Obedience to God is a way to display your love for Him. You love God because He first loved you. Jesus submitted to the will of the Father when He chose to die on a cross for you and I. He chose to give up His rights and His wants in order to do what the Father wanted for Him. Jesus did not question whether or not to submit His will to the Father, He chose obedience. Obedience is not simply agreeing with a directive, it is about taking action that aligns with the directive. God wants you to trust Him with your life and obey His instruction even when you do not understand why or feel like obeying. By obeying God, you are demonstrating your faithfulness and love to Him. You obey His commands, not because you have to, but because you want to and are able to. Through your obedience to God, you can grow closer to Him and know His will for you. God knows what is best for you and you are to trust in Him so that you can be used for Him and His purpose.

Reflection: Am I being obedient to God or obedient to my sin nature?

Prayer: Lord, I pray that You renew my strength to resist temptation and obey Your Word. Help me to trust in You alone and be obedient to Your commands and Your will. Amen

Obedience [oh-bee-dee-uh ns]

the act or practice of obeying; dutiful or submissive compliance:

John 14:23
Jesus replied, "Anyone who loves me will obey my teaching. My Father will love them, and we will come to them and make our home with them.

Ephesians 6:1-3
Children, obey your parents in the Lord, for this is right. "Honor your father and mother"—which is the first commandment with a promise— "so that it may go well with you and that you may enjoy long life on the earth."

John 14:21
Whoever has my commands and keeps them is the one who loves me. The one who loves me will be loved by my Father, and I too will love them and show myself to them."

Romans 6:16
Don't you know that when you offer yourselves to someone as obedient slaves, you are slaves of the one you obey—whether you are slaves to sin, which leads to death, or to obedience, which leads to righteousness?

James 1:22
Do not merely listen to the word, and so deceive yourselves. Do what it says.

Isaiah 1:19
If you are willing and obedient, you will eat the good things of the land;

1 Samuel 15:22
But Samuel replied: "Does the Lord delight in burnt offerings and sacrifices as much as in obeying the Lord? To obey is better than sacrifice, and to heed is better than the fat of rams.

Titus 3:1
Remind the people to be subject to rulers and authorities, to be obedient, to be ready to do whatever is good,

Hebrews 5:8
Son though he was, he learned obedience from what he suffered

2 Corinthians 2:9
Another reason I wrote you was to see if you would stand the test and be obedient in everything.

Luke 6:46
"Why do you call me, 'Lord, Lord,' and do not do what I say?

2 Corinthians 5:17
Therefore, if anyone is in Christ, the new creation has come:[a] The old has gone, the new is here!

Proverbs 6:20
My son, keep your father's command and do not forsake your mother's teaching.

BE OBEDIENT EVEN WHEN YOU
DO NOT KNOW WHERE
OBEDIENCE MAY LEAD YOU.
-SINCLAIR FERGUSON

OBEDIENCE

is not the mark of a slave; it is
one of the prime qualities of

LEADERSHIP

Faith [feyth]

strong or unshakeable belief in something, esp without proof or evidence

From the time I was 5 years old, I pursued many wrestling goals. Whether it was to win an elementary AAU tournament, a high school championship or a collegiate national championship, I pursued after each goal passionately. I spent countless hours training and perfecting my technique and conditioning. I did not know for sure if I would ever accomplish those goals. I encountered many failures and setbacks along the way. I believed in the work that I was putting in and I had hope that it would all work out in the end. But what kept me going was more than hope. It was faith. Faith is having a confidence and trust in something. I had faith in myself, my training, my coaches and God that I could achieve my goals.

For me, having faith in myself, my training and my coaches gave me a reason to continue to push and truly believe that I could achieve my goals. There was no guarantee or certainty that I would meet my goals but I had faith that I could. I was confident that the work that I was putting in and the instruction I was receiving would lead me to the outcome I desired no matter how many obstacles were in my way. My faith in God helped to keep life and sports in a proper perspective. My identity was not in whether I won or lost, but rather on who God said I was. My faith in God helped take the focus off of me and onto Him. I found that it reduced anxiety and stress and increased my confidence. I believed that God was in control and whatever happened was supposed to happen and it was for my benefit and His glory. That included whether I won or lost. I don't know if God cares about sports but I believe He cares about you. God has blessed you with talent and abilities and there are many platforms that you can use those talents to reach others for His purpose.

Faith is important because it affects the decisions that you make, the way that you interact with others and the way you react to situations. In both sports and life, what you believe affects who you are and what you do. The bible says in Colossians 3:17, "And whatever you do, whether in word or deed, do it all in the name of the Lord Jesus, giving thanks to God the father through him." In anything that you do, you can do it for the Glory of God versus your own glory. God gets the glory when you perform your tasks to the best of your ability and doing it in a way that pleases Him. People are always watching and how you live out your faith matters. Choose to honor God with your life and your actions. Trust in His ways, seek His character and have faith in God's promises. No matter what circumstances you face, you can have confidence that your faith in Jesus will overcome any obstacle in your path and will never fail you. When you place your faith and trust in Christ alone for your salvation, God forgives your sins and sees only the righteousness of Christ on your behalf ensuring your eternal salvation. Have faith in God's Word, His provisions and have faith in Jesus Christ as your personal savior. Be willing to act out your faith in your daily life. Make God the center of your life, keep the faith and watch God work in your life.

Reflection: What areas of my life am I withholding from God? Is God my first priority and am I living a life centered around Him? Do I trust God enough to act on my faith?

Prayer: Lord, strengthen my faith. Help me to make You the center of my life. Help me to trust and seek You in every area. Let me trust You and be able to act out my faith without fear or worry. Help my faith be unshakeable. Amen.

"He answered, "'Love the Lord your God with all your heart and with all your soul and with all your strength and with all your mind'; and, 'Love your neighbor as yourself.'
- Luke 10:27

Faith [feyth]

strong or unshakeable belief in something, esp without proof or evidence

Hebrews 11:1
Now faith is confidence in what we hope for and assurance about what we do not see.

Ephesians 2:8-9
For it is by grace you have been saved, through faith—and this is not from yourselves, it is the gift of God— not by works, so that no one can boast.

John 3:16
For God so loved the world that he gave his one and only Son, that whoever believes in him shall not perish but have eternal life.

Galatians 3:26
So in Christ Jesus you are all children of God through faith

Matthew 21:22
If you believe, you will receive whatever you ask for in prayer."

Hebrews 11:6
And without faith it is impossible to please God, because anyone who comes to him must believe that he exists and that he rewards those who earnestly seek him.

Proverbs 3:5-6
Trust in the Lord with all your heart and lean not on your own understanding; in all your ways submit to him, and he will make your paths straight.

1 Corinthians 2:5
so that your faith might not rest on human wisdom, but on God's power.

2 Corinthians 5:7
For we live by faith, not by sight.

1 Corinthians 13:13
And now these three remain: faith, hope and love. But the greatest of these is love.

2 Timothy 4:7
I have fought the good fight, I have finished the race, I have kept the faith.

1 Peter 1:8-9
Though you have not seen him, you love him; and even though you do not see him now, you believe in him and are filled with an inexpressible and glorious joy, 9 for you are receiving the end result of your faith, the salvation of your souls.

James 1:3
because you know that the testing of your faith produces perseverance.

2 Corinthians 4:18
So we fix our eyes not on what is seen, but on what is unseen, since what is seen is temporary, but what is unseen is eternal.

FAITH
"IT'S ALL ABOUT BELIEVING, YOU DON'T KNOW HOW IT WILL HAPPEN, BUT YOU KNOW IT WILL."

FAITH IS TAKING THE FIRST STEP EVEN WHEN YOU CAN'T SEE THE WHOLE STAIRCASE.

-MARTIN LUTHER KING JR.

FAITH IS NOT
KNOWING
WHAT THE FUTURE
HOLDS,
BUT KNOWING
WHO HOLDS THE
FUTURE.

The Mental Edge:
How I Approached Match Preparation

One of the most overused clichés in sports is that 90 percent of performance is mental. The reality of that statement is that I believe it to be 100% true. How you approach a match from a mental perspective is as important as or more important than how you have physically trained for the match. When I was younger, I struggled with my mental preparation. I was worried about who my opponent was and who they had beaten before. I would wrestle my opponents differently depending on who I thought they were or how good I thought they were. I would get anxiety and be stressed out which led to a negative snowball effect. I would warm up too soon or too much and be exhausted before I ever walked out on the mat. I would have self-doubt and worry which led to panic and my body fatiguing faster than it should have. Nervousness and fear of losing would consume my mind. All of these negative side effects were a result of poor mental preparation and prevented me from wrestling to my true potential. I believe that many athletes go through similar struggles. What changed? How did I overcome these struggles?

For me, I had to approach each match like I did practice. I did not experience any of the anxiety, stress, nervousness or other negative side effects when I went to practice each day. In practice, I could go hard the entire hour or two hours of practice in drilling and live wrestling without experiencing the major body fatigue that I would experience in a short seven minute live match. I was convinced that the only difference between practice and live matches was my mental approach. I did not panic in practice if I was taken down. I had no fear of losing in the practice room. How could I go hard the entire practice but get so exhausted during an actual match? I had to change my mindset. I had to treat my live matches the same way that I treated practice. I treated practice as work and I trained myself to approach live matches as work. I had a job to do and my only focus was the tasks at hand. My sole goal was to go out and punch my time clock. To do my job. I focused on the little things like my footwork, my set-ups, my takedowns, my escapes and my turns. I tried to focus only on the things that I could control. I tried to constantly be working and scoring. My job was to work for the fall. If I could not get the pin, I would work for the technical fall. If I could not get the technical fall, I would work for the major decision. If I could not get the major decision, I would work for the win. The win was the fourth thing on my list of priorities. With this approach, if I set the bar high and failed, I still succeeded and got the win. I think many wrestlers walk out on the mat hoping to get a win. If that is their starting point then the next step down would be a loss. Many wrestlers approach their matches not to lose. Their fear of failure prevents them from opening up on the mat. I approached my matches to dominate. I wanted to go out and pin every kid that I wrestled. If I was working for the pin then that meant I was scoring points which helped me to secure the win. I no longer cared about who my opponent was or what their record was. For me, they became faceless and nameless people that were just an obstacle in my way to achieving my goals. I had a job to do and it did not matter who was standing across the line from me. They were trying to prevent me from reaching my goals. The only way that I believe that you can have that mental approach is by earning it. You have to earn it with how hard you work. You have to put the time in and train. I felt that I worked harder and sacrificed more than everyone else and that I deserved it more. Whether I actually harder than everyone else or not, that did not matter. I believed I did. Belief and confidence are strong traits that are required to have the mental edge. That belief and confidence comes from experience. In practice, I was willing to put myself in uncomfortable situations and learned to battle out of them. Because I trained for those situations, I was able to stay calm, poised and confident that I was able to wrestle out of those positions in a live match. They say you perform how you practice and that could not be more true for me. Lastly, I think it is important to make sure that you keep sports and your performance in a proper perspective. Stop worrying about what people may think or say about your performance and go out and give your best effort. Wins and losses do not define who you are, God does. He has blessed you with athletic talents so be thankful and use them to reach others for Him. Wrestling is just a platform that allows you to display His character and His gifts that you have been blessed with. Win or lose, your attitude, your effort and your character speaks more to others than any trophy ever will. Stay humble, stay hungry, work hard and never give up.

"BE HUMBLE. BE HUNGRY. AND ALWAYS BE THE HARDEST WORKER IN THE ROOM."

-DWAYNE "THE ROCK" JOHNSON

EVERY CHAMPION WAS
ONCE A CONTENDER
THAT *REFUSED*
TO GIVE UP

-ROCKY BALBOA

I HATED EVERY MINUTE
OF TRAINING, BUT I SAID,
"DON'T QUIT. SUFFER NOW
AND LIVE THE REST OF YOUR
LIFE AS A CHAMPION."
- MUHAMMAD ALI

Top Ten Ways To Be Champion

1. **Remember your gifts come from GOD...Stay humble and work for excellence**
   a. "I can do everything through him who gives me strength" Philippians 4:13
   b. "It is God who arms me with strength and makes my way perfect. He makes my feet like the feet of a deer; he enables me to stand on the heights. He trains my hands for battle; my arms can bend a bow of bronze. You give me your shield of victory; you stoop down to make me great." 2 Samuel 22:33

2. **Keep your weight under control**
   a. Eat right and maintain your weight. Put in the extra workouts. Don't starve yourself. Eat healthy and have self-control.

3. **Winning starts with your attitude and confidence...BELIEVE in yourself**
   a. When you step on the mat you have to believe that you can win. Wrestle your match and your style. Make them try to stop your best stuff.
   b. Hit your moves and setups like you believe that they will work. Don't do anything halfway.
   c. Stay positive even with adversity or a defeat. Learn from it and work harder to overcome it.

4. **Always work harder than everyone else**
   a. Push yourself farther than your body can go and it will respond.
   b. When you don't feel like you can go any farther, keep going. Push your limits.

5. **REFUSE to lose**
   a. NEVER give up. You are never out of a match until you allow your mind to give up. It is not over until that last buzzer.

6. **Be a LEADER on and off the mat**
   a. Lead by example with your work ethic and self-discipline.
   b. Winning is contagious and it will affect the team.

7. **Allow yourself to be open-minded and continue to learn**
   a. There is always someone better than you. You must continue learning technique and taking instruction. You must be Coachable.

8. **You've got to want it**
   a. Nobody else can wrestle the match for you or train for you. Don't rely on others to push you. YOU have got to want it for YOURSELF, not mom or dad, your brother or your coaches, but for yourself. Find your "Why" and let it drive you.

9. **Hold each other accountable**
   a. This is a team sport so help your teammates out and hold them responsible for their actions. You only get better by wrestling better kids. So make your teammates better.

10. **Finish the season with NO REGRETS**
    a. Don't look back on your season and say...if only I did this or if only I worked a little harder or if only I took it more seriously or I will get them next year. There may not be a next year or another opportunity like this.
    b. Give it your all 100% of the time and have the self-discipline and will-power to see it through
    c. Win or lose be able to honestly say to yourself that you did all that you could and there was nothing more I could do to be better. That's how you become a CHAMPION.

Preparing for Battle: A Wrestler's Prayer

2 Samuel 33-40

"It is God who arms me with strength and makes my way perfect.	FAITH/TRUST/BELIEF
He makes my feet like the feet of a deer; he enables me to stand on the heights.	SPEED/QUICKNESS
He trains my hands for battle; my arms can bend a bow of bronze.	STRENGTH/STAMINA
You give me your shield of victory; you stoop down to make me great.	PROTECTION/DEFENSE
You broaden the path beneath me, so that my ankles do not turn.	HEALTH/SAFETY
"I pursued my enemies and crushed them; I did not turn back till they were destroyed.	INTENSITY/RELENTLESS ATTACK
I crushed them completely, and they could not rise; they fell beneath my feet.	DOMINATION/MENTAL TOUGHNESS
You armed me with strength for battle; you made my adversaries bow at my feet."	PREPARATION VICTORY!!!

Win or lose, glorify the Lord with your effort.

"Lord, I recognize that all my blessings come from You and I thank You for my talents and gifts. I pray that You make my feet light and quick and that You give my body strength and endurance. I pray for safety and protection from injury for both me and my opponent. I pray that my mind is clear, focused and resolved to finish strong and fight to the very end. I pray for victory but win or lose today, I pray that You get the glory. I pray that my attitude and actions glorify You today in victory or defeat. Thank you, Amen."

HAVE I NOT COMMANDED YOU?

BE STRONG AND COURAGEOUS.

DO NOT BE AFRAID; DO NOT BE DISCOURAGED, FOR THE LORD YOUR GOD WILL BE WITH YOU WHEREVER YOU GO.

FAITH

BUILDING

"For I delivered to you as of first importance what I also received: that Christ died for our sins in accordance with the Scriptures, that he was buried, that he was raised on the third day in accordance with the Scriptures."

-1 Corinthians 15:3-4

Complexity of Your World

You were likely taught in school that the world began through the Big Bang Theory and that humans and animals are a result of evolution. You were not taught about intelligent design and creationism in school. So when faced with the Bible, you start to question, "How can the Bible say one thing but education and science be saying another"? This great divide causes you to question God and His Word and it draws a hard line between religion and science. However, there are many scholars who do believe in creationism and believe that God was the creator of the universe. My goal with this writing is to simply cause you to ask questions and give thoughts to God based on creation itself.

There is great debate on how the world and everything began. Was it the Big Bang Theory where everything exploded and then formed by chance of nature? Was it by a divine being or by an intelligent designer? Did humans and animals evolve through natural selection or was it through divine creation? Many people are divided. I believe that God created the heavens and the earth just as it is described in the Bible. For me, there are too many things in nature that I do not believe could have happened by chance. The complexities of nature and the many systems and cycles are evidence enough to me that something more intelligent and far beyond human understanding is at work.

Let's just examine earth itself. Did mankind just get very lucky or is there an intelligent plan in place when it comes to our planet. The tilt of earth is exactly 23.5 degrees which allows the four seasons to occur. If it was tilted any more or any less, temperatures would be too extreme and many parts of earth would be uninhabitable. The earth rotates every 24 hours like clockwork on itself and takes 365 days to rotate around the sun. It is a completely stable and controlled phenomenon that remains consistent day after day and year after year. The distance of earth from the sun allows the earth's surface temperature to be suitable for life. A distance too close or too far would again cause Earth to be uninhabitable. The Earth's atmosphere has just the right composition and density of gases to sustain life. Earth is the only known planet to have water in liquid form. The chemical and physical properties of liquid water are necessary for life to survive and the world ocean regulates the earth's temperature and serves as a reservoir for many important chemicals. If you just look at these scientific facts, it indicates either that an intelligent designer planned and designed this amazing planet, or that it originated by a fortuitous accident. To me, you only have two choices, one must decide either God or by chance.

You see complexities throughout life. Look at the human body and it's incredible internal systems. Your DNA and cellular structure, circulatory and immune systems, digestive and nervous system, your muscular and skeletal systems are all scientifically extraordinary and complicated. Look at the reproductive systems of a male and female so that humans can procreate. Did those parts just happen to evolve at the same time on a male and a female? These same systems also exist in animals of all kinds. Did all of these extraordinary systems just develop by evolution and by random chance? The complexities of your body have to point to an intelligent designer. If you look in detail at each one of these amazing systems, could they have evolved from just a single-cell organism over time like many scholars theorize?

Look at the cellular structure of plants and trees, the water cycle, the seasons, the carbon cycle and nitrogen cycle and the general order of many things in nature. Is it a coincidence that humans breathe out carbon dioxide, and plants absorb it? Yet, through photosynthesis, plants release oxygen which humans need to breathe for survival. Did that also happen by chance? Was structure and order in all of these areas somehow formed out of a mass explosion and chaos? Did nature just somehow know how to organize itself in such a systematic way? Or, is there a divine and all-knowing God that designed it that way?

Complexity of Your World

If you think you live in a big world, the universe is unimaginably larger than your mind can probably comprehend. If you look at the vastness of the universe and the sheer size and distance of known stars and galaxies it truly is mind boggling. How did those stars and galaxies get there and how are there so many of them? Did you know that it takes one year for the Earth to rotate the Sun but it takes 225 million years for the Sun to rotate the Milky Way galaxy? Did you know that there are about 7.2 billion people on Earth? There are nearly 28 times more stars in the galaxy than there are people and there are over 200 billion galaxies in the observable universe! Light travels at an astonishing 186,000 miles a second. One light-year is about 5.88 trillion miles. VV Cephei is one of the largest known stars located in the constellation Cepheus, approximately 5,000 light years from Earth. According to science, that would be close to thirty trillion miles away! VV Cephei has a radius of about 1.55 billion miles. That makes it 382,000 times larger than Earth in radius. Try to imagine Earth as one millimeter which is little less than half an inch. Now compare that to about 680 feet or roughly 2.25 football fields. That is the size of the earth's diameter compared to the size of VV Cephei star's diameter! How could an explosion from a "Big Bang" send such massive objects so far away from each other? An explosion sent a star that is 1.55 billion miles in diameter over 30 trillion miles away? As far as science can observe and prove, the universe has no beginning and no end. Why is it that if you can observe actual creation that has no beginning and no end, that it is so difficult to believe God's Word telling you that God is eternal with no beginning and no end? The Bible says, "In the beginning God created the heavens and the earth". That He is "the Alpha and the Omega, who is and who was, and who is to come". Isaiah 40:28 says, "Do you not know? Have you not heard? The Lord is the everlasting God, the Creator of the ends of the earth". How was Moses, the author of Genesis ever to know that science would observe a universe so vast when he wrote the words in Genesis? Were all of the billions of stars, galaxies and planets created by a random explosion or could it be an eternal God and the works of His hands that created it all?

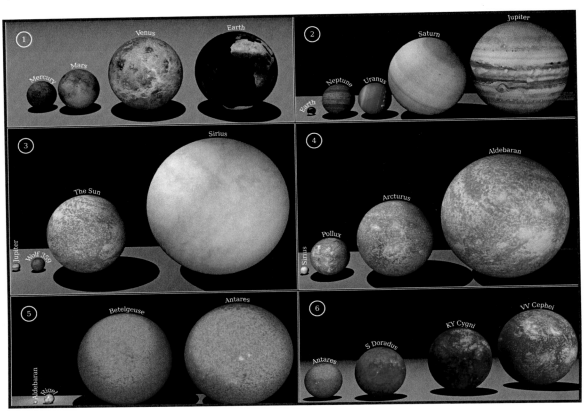

The Bible: A Unique Book

The Bible is indeed a very unique book. The facts of the Bible cannot be explained solely by human theories concerning its origin. The Bible itself claims that it is unique among all books and is God's Word to humanity. It has had more influence in the world than any other book. It has withstood over 2000 years of intense scrutiny by critics and has maintained its credibility throughout history. The Bible has been translated into over 2300 languages and is the world's best seller. There are over 100 million Bibles sold or given away every year in the world. Why is the Bible so powerful and popular but yet so controversial?

The Bible claims to be the inspired Word of God. The Bible contains 66 books that were written by 43 men over a span of 1600 years yet is completely consistent throughout. We can't tell 10 people the same thing in 10 minutes and get the same story. Yet the bible shares the same message with consistency despite being written by men at times of war, at times of peace, by rulers and kings, by fishermen, by Jesus and many more. How could such marvelous continuity been achieved without divine guidance? The scriptures claim to be the very words of God. 2 Timothy 3:16 says, "All scripture is God-breathed".

The Bible claims to be without error. Inerrancy means that when all facts are known, the Scriptures in their original autographs and properly interpreted will be shown to be wholly true in everything that they affirm. There are tens of thousands of details in the Bible that could be either confirmed or disproved by history, archaeology, science, and more. Yet, only the Bible contains detailed prophecies about the coming Savior of the world, prophecies which have proven true in history.

It is not only a book outlining historical events but it is also an instruction manual as the revealed Word of God. It teaches of how you may come to know God personally and how you are to conduct yourself morally. It defines what your purpose is and claims to explain the origins of life. Only the Bible begins with the creation of the universe and lays out a historical record of mankind to the end of times.

The entire Bible is about one central figure – Jesus Christ. The complete Old Testament points to a coming redeemer through stories, metaphors or direct prophecies. The New Testament shows the fulfillment of these prophecies through Jesus Christ and the meaning as well as the consequences of His coming.

What the Bible teaches is that the one true God sent His only Son, Jesus, to die for your sins so that you can inherit eternal life as a free gift. Salvation is not something you can earn. It is only through your belief in Jesus's death, burial and ressurrection that you can be saved from an eternal separation from God. This is a profound claim that forces a reader to make a decision on whether to reject or accept the claim. This is a personal decision that every person that hears His word must make. If the Bible is true, no other personal decision a person makes will be more consequential than their decision to accept or reject God's invitation for salvation through Jesus.

"For it is by grace you have been saved, through faith—and this is not from yourselves, it is the gift of God— not by works, so that no one can boast."
- Ephesians 2:8-9

"If you declare with your mouth, "Jesus is Lord," and believe in your heart that God raised him from the dead, you will be saved. For it is with your heart that you believe and are justified, and it is with your mouth that you profess your faith and are saved".
- Romans 10:9-10

Archaeological Evidence

Is the Bible true? For thousands of years, skeptics have tried to disprove the authenticity of the Bible. Yet, time after time, the more they search for evidence to support their claims, the more they find archaeological evidence of people, places and things mentioned in the Bible that are historically accurate.

The discovery of artifacts, ruins, historical documents and cities that are mentioned in the Bible are evidence that the Bible is not just stories but historical accounts. The discovery of artifacts like the Dead Sea Scrolls in 1947 demonstrates the accuracy that the Bible we have today is virtually the same Bible as the one more than 2000 years ago. The Dead Sea Scrolls contained over 800 scrolls and fragments that contain practicaly the entire Old Testament. Ignoring spelling-oriented changes and similar small differences, the Dead Sea Scrolls matched the Hebrew text of today's Old Testament. This is in spite of the fact that over 2,000 years had passed. In addition, there are over 20,000 known manuscripts documenting the New Testament text. This makes the New Testament the most reliable document of antiquity in existence.

Another recent archaeological discovery of significance occurred in 1993. A broken fragment of basalt stone was uncovered that referenced King David. This is significant becuase it provides an archaeological connection to the ruling dynasty established by King David of the Bible.

The Ossuary of Caiaphas, a stone bone box for burial was discovered in 1990 that referred to Joseph son of Caiaphas. Caiaphas was whom Jesus was brought for questioning in Matthew 26:3 and 57, and Luke 3:2 as well as mentioned in the book of John and Acts.

Pontius Pilate's historical existence has been affirmed. In addition to being mentioned by secular historians like Josephus, Philo and Tacitus, Pontius Pilate also had coins issued during his governance that have been discovered. Plus, in 1961, an inscription was discovered that affirmed his title as governor.

In Genesis 23 and Samuel 11, the Bible refers to the Hittites. In 1906, archaeologists discovered ruins of Hattusas, the ancient Hittite capital as well as a vast collection of Hittite historical records that dated back to the mid-second millennium BC. Prior to this, historians believed that the Hittite people did not exist.

Discoveries of ancient Bible cities like Jericho, Babylon, Dan, Shiloh, Megiddo and a dozen others also provide evidence of the Bible's Old Testament accounts and historical accuracy.

The Old Testament was written between approximately 1450 BC and 430 BC. During that time, many predictions of the future were recorded in the Bible by God's prophets. Of the events that were to have taken place by now, many have happened just the way the Bible predicted it would. Whether it was the prophecies of Jesus or prophecies like the account of Nebuchadnezzar, the fall of Tyre, the prophecies of Jericho, Palestine, Moab and Babylon, the plowing of Mount Zion and many more, historians can look back on these predictions and see that the prophecies actually came true just as the Bible predicted them to hundreds of years before.

These discoveries are only a small sample of the archaeological evidence that point to the truth that the Bible is historically accurate and not just fictional stories. We may never be able to prove every claim of the Bible, but we can look at many pieces of evidence that supports its validity. The above discoveries are only a small sample of the evidence that is available that point to the truth of the Bible. There is much more evidence to consider. I encourage you to examine the evidence and make your own decisions. I think you will find that it points you to a greater TRUTH.

Stories That Point to Jesus

God uses humans to tell His story and accomplish His will. In the Old Testament, God used man to point to Jesus as the coming redeemer. The stories in the Old Testament are historical accounts which paint pictures of the coming Messiah. The entire Old Testament tells of stories that point to a coming redeemer which God promises in Genesis 3:15. The stories that you have heard as children have more meaning than you may first realize. Noah and the flood and the one door in the ark represents only one way to be saved. The sacrificial ram of Abraham and Isaac is a picture of Christ sacrificing himself for you. The Bronze serpent and the Israelites is a picture of Christ being lifted up on the Cross and you simply needing to believe in Him to be saved, just as the Israelites had to look at the bronze serpent to be healed from the poisonous vipers. The story of the Passover points to the power of the blood of the lamb to conquer death. Jesus is the sacrificial lamb and His blood is the only way that you can be saved. David and Goliath is story of a mere servant boy who became the savior of the Israelites by conquering a giant that they could not defeat on their own, just as Christ is your savior that defeats sin and death for you today. Is it just coincidence that all of these real life stories draw significant parallels to Jesus's life and point to Him as the coming redeemer? Or, could it be that God's hand was orchestrating these events all along so that you could now look back and read about them and believe?

Noah and the Flood

The story of Noah and the flood is about God's wrath and his provisions for those that believe His Word. Noah trusted and obeyed God to build the ark even though it did not make sense from a human perspective. The ark had one door and only those that entered through that one door were saved from complete destruction when the flood waters came. Noah and his family believed God's Word and they were saved. Just like the story of Noah and the flood, you too have a choice. You have a choice to believe God and His Word and trust in Jesus. If you choose to ignore or disbelieve God's Word then you may face God's wrath. God's Word says there is only one way to salvation in John 14:6, "I am the way, the truth, and the life. No one can come to the Father except through me." Jesus is the only way and the one door to salvation that you must enter through. Believe God's Word and accept Jesus as your personal savior so you can spend eternity with God.

Abraham & Isaac

Abraham loved his son, Isaac. God tested Abraham to see if Abraham worshipped God alone above all earthly things. Abraham was asked to sacrifice his one and only son. Abraham committed to trust God and obey, but God intervened and provided a substitutional sacrifice instead of Isaac. He provided a male ram that was caught in the bushes by its horns. Isaac was spared and the ram took his place on the altar. The story about Abraham and Isaac points to the sacrifice of Jesus. Isaac was helpless to save himself and was about to die before God intervened and provided a ram in his place. The same is true for you today. You are destined to hell but God intervened and provided Jesus as that atoning sacrifice in your place. The punishment of sin is death. You are guilty but Jesus took your place and your punishment for you just like the ram took the place for Isaac. God provided His one and only son, Jesus, to take the punishment for your past, present and future sins so that you can spend eternity with him.

Stories That Point to Jesus

The Passover

The Israelites were enslaved by the Egyptians. God had provided many plagues over Eqypt in an effort to change the Pharaoh's heart to let the Israelites go free. The last plague was the plague of death of the first born. The angel of death would come in the night and those that did not believe God's Word and obey His commands would suffer the death of the first born in each family. God provided specific instructions to the Israelites the night before their Exodus from slavery in Egypt. To be spared from the plague, it required a lamb to be killed and the blood of the lamb to be placed onto the door-posts of their homes. When the angel of Death passed by that night, those that had the sacrificial blood of the lamb were spared and those that did not died. God kept His Word and the Israelites were set free. This is a picture of Christ's blood shed on the cross for you. It is the only way to salvation. Only those that believe in Jesus and trust in His blood alone will have eternal salvation and will be set free from the punishments of sin and death. Salvation comes from trusting in the blood of Jesus. All of those that do not believe will spend eternity separated from God.

The Bronze Serpent

After the Israelites exodus from Egypt the Israelites wandered the desert. While the Israelites were in the desert, they began to grumble against God. God sent venomous serpents as judgment against the people for their sin. God directed Moses to put a bronze serpent on a pole. The bronze serpent on the stick was a reminder of their sin which brought upon their suffering. Moses instructed the Israelites that if anyone was bitten by the serpent they merely had to look at the bronze serpent on the cross to be healed. God was teaching the Israelites a lesson about faith. There was nothing they could do on their own to be healed but believe God's Word. Today, you look to Jesus and His death on the cross to be healed from your sin which leads to eternal death. Like the snake, Jesus became sin when He took His place on the cross and died for your salvation. Jesus died for payment of your sin. Just like the bronze serpent, you must simply look to Jesus and believe to have eternal life. It is your faith in Jesus alone that saves you.

David & Goliath

Goliath stood over 9 feet tall and was covered with bronze armor and weapons. He taunted the Israelites for 40 days. The Israelites were helpless to defeat such an enemy. To defeat the Philistines, the Israelites had to choose one man to fight Goliath one on one. Based on whoever won the battle, the loser would become servants to the winner. David was a mere shepherd boy and servant who trusted God. He volunteered to fight Goliath. A mere boy versus a 9 foot giant. He was outmatched and outsized by Goliath. Yet he trusted in God and was able to slay the mighty giant and save the Israelites with a few small stones. David became the savior of Israelites when they were helpless to save themselves. Today, you also cannot help yourself from the giant enemy of sin and death. You need a champion savior to represent you and save you from your sin. That champion is Jesus who took your place and conquered sin and death. Just like David's victory was the Israelites victory, Jesus's victory on the cross is also your victory today when you trust in Him.

Prophecies Fulfilled

Have you ever heard the phrase, "Hindsight is 20/20"? It is a phrase used to describe the fact that it is easy for one to be knowledgeable about an event after it has happened. Well when it comes to the Bible, we really do have that advantage. We can look at history to see what the Bible said and then compare it to what really happened. This may be one of the most powerful pieces of evidence to show that the Bible really was inspired by God. The Bible contains hundreds of prophecies from God that were written down hundreds of years before their fulfillment. These are events that have already occurred and can be documented in history, both by the Bible and in secular writings. Prophecy fulfillment is powerful evidence that validates the credibility and supernatural inspiration of the Old Testament.

The Bible reveals several prophecies foretelling the life and mission of the Messiah, Jesus Christ. Jesus Christ fulfilled over 300 prophecies alone regarding his life, death and resurrection that were predicted 500 to 1000 years before He was even born. These prophecies foretold what to look for in the coming Messiah in great details. Prophecies that foretold of the town that the Messiah would be born in, the lineage He would come from, what His characteristics would be like, how He would be treated, how He would be betrayed, His manner of death, His burial location and how He would rise again. The odds of one man fulfilling just 8 of the 300 prophecies that Jesus Christ fulfilled in the Bible are astronomical. A probability study that Dr. John Stoner conducted puts the odds at 1 in 100 trillion! That is 1×10^{28}. To put that number in perspective, imagine filling the entire state of Texas up knee deep in silver dollars with one silver dollar marked with a black check mark. Then, turn a blindfolded person loose in this sea of silver dollars and calculate the odds that the first coin he or she would pick up would be the one with the black check mark. Those extremely low odds are the same odds that 8 prophecies were fulfilled accidentally in the life of Jesus. The 1 in 100 trillion odds are only if 8 of the prophecies were fulfilled by one person. Jesus fulfilled nearly 300 prophecies! If the Bible was written by man, how could that possibly be? Did the prophets just get lucky over and over again? The only explanation that I can believe is that God inspired the writers just as He said and only He knows what the future holds with such accuracy.

When you look at the Old Testament prophecies and you compare Jesus to what the prophecies say to look for in the coming redeemer, then you have to conclude that Jesus Christ certainly fit the description. The prophecies of the Old Testament and the fulfillment of the prophecies in the New Testament points to Jesus as the Messiah. Jesus fits the "fingerprint" of the prophecies in a manner that nobody else ever did or will be able to do in the future. He is the Messiah that mankind was searching for.

Jesus himself claimed He was fulfilling prophecy. In the Sermon on the Mount in Matthew 5:17, Jesus said, "Do not think that I have come to abolish the Law or the Prophets; I have not come to abolish them but to fulfill them". After His resurrection Jesus spoke to the disciples saying, "This is what I told you while I was still with you: Everything must be fulfilled that is written about Me in the Law of Moses, the Prophets and the Psalms (Luke 24:44)!"

The prophecies are not exclusive to the coming Messiah. We find multiple accounts of secular prophecies concerning cities and nations that were foretold years before they actually happened. The account of Nebuchadnezzar, the fall of Tyre, the prophecies of Jericho, Palestine, Moab and Babylon, the plowing of Mount Zion are just a few.

How could all of these prophecies come true just as it was written? Is Jesus the real Messiah that the Bible predicted would come to save mankind? Or, were the prophets just really good guessers? Maybe, God is who He says He is.

Prophecies Fulfilled

Was Jesus really the Promised Redeemer? Jesus fulfilled over 300 prophecies about the coming Savior that were predicted hundreds of years before. Here are just 16 of them.

PROPHECIES ABOUT CHRIST'S LIFE, DEATH AND RESURRECTION

the Lord himself will give you the sign. Look! The virgin will conceive a child! - Isaiah 7:14	**Born of A Virgin** (740-680 BC)	*while she was still a virgin, she became pregnant through the power of the Holy Spirit.* - Matthew 1:18-25
But you, O Bethlehem...Yet a ruler of Israel,... will come from you on my behalf. - Micah 5:2	**Born in Bethlehem** (735-710 BC)	*Jesus was born in Bethlehem in Judea, during the reign of King Herod.* - Matthew 2:1
When Israel was a child, I loved him, and I called my son out of Egypt. - Hosea 11:1	**Flee into Egypt** (750 BC)	*That night Joseph left for Egypt with the child and Mary, his mother,* - Matthew 2:14
Look, your king is coming to you. He is righteous and victorious,...riding on a donkey - Zech 9:9	**Jerusalem on a donkey** (480-470 BC)	*They brought the donkey and the colt to him and ... and he sat on it* - Matthew 21:6-8
Even my best friend, the one I trusted completely... has turned against me. - Psalm 41:9	**Betrayed by a friend** (1020-970 BC)	*Then Judas Iscariot, ..went to the leading priests to arrange to betray Jesus to them.* - Mark 14:10-11
So they counted out for my wages thirty pieces of silver. - Zecharia 11:12-13	**Sold for 30 pieces of silver** (480-470 BC)	*"How much will you pay? ...And they gave him thirty pieces of silver.* - Matthew 26:14-15
He was oppressed and treated harshly, yet he never said a word. - Isaiah 53:7	**Silent when accused** (740-680 BC)	*Pilate asked him, "Aren't you going to answer them? ...but Jesus said nothing* - Mark 15:3-5
We turned our backs on him and looked the other way...we did not care. - Isaiah 53:3	**Rejected by the Jews** (740-680 BC)	*what should I do with this man you call the king of the Jews?"..."Crucify him!"* - Mark 15:9-14
They have pierced my hands and feet. - Psalm 22:16	**Hands & feet pierced** (1020-970 BC)	*Then the soldiers nailed him to the cross.* - Mark 15:24
They divide my garments among themselves and throw dice for my clothing - Psalm 22:18	**Clothes gambled for** (1020-970 BC)	*They divided his clothes and threw dice to decide who would get each piece.* - Mark 15:24
He was beaten so we could be whole. He was whipped so we could be healed. - Isaiah 53:5	**Beaten and Whipped** (740-680 BC)	*Then Pilate had Jesus flogged with a lead-tipped whip.* - John 19:1-2
He was counted among the rebels. He bore the sins of many. - Isaiah 53:12	**Die with the wicked** (740-680 BC)	*Two revolutionaries were crucified with him, one on his right and one on his left.* - Mark 15:27
"In that day," ..."I will make the sun go down at noon and darken the earth ... - Amos 8:9	**Darkness** (760 BC)	*At noon, darkness fell across the whole land until three o'clock* - Matthew 27:45
But he was buried like a criminal; he was put in a rich man's grave. - Isaiah 53:9	**Buried with the rich** (740-680 BC)	*Joseph of Arimathea took a risk and went to Pilate.. ...he took Jesus' body ...laid it in a tomb.* - Mark 15:43-46
you will not leave my soul among the dead...to rot in the grave. - Psalm 16:10	**Rise again** (1020-970 BC)	*He isn't here! He is risen from the dead! Remember what he told you back in Galilee,* - Luke 24:6
When you ascended to the heights, you led a crowd of captives. - Psalm 68:18	**Go back to Heaven** (970-610 BC)	*he was taken up into a cloud while they were watching, and they could no longer see him.* - Acts 1:9

Personal Experience

Personal experience is very subjective, meaning it is just one person's point of view. There really isn't any concrete proof or objective evidence that you can gather from someone's personal experience, especially when it comes to the topic of God. Personal experience is that person's interpretation of the experience. But, personal experience is very real and powerful for the person involved. I am only offering my perspective and my experience with Jesus as encouragement to help strengthen your faith.

Growing up, I was not raised in the church or really knew much about God. I always felt that there was something more and a mightier power at work but really didn't think much about it. I did well in school and had a good childhood and had a lot of success in sports and academically. It was not until college that I really started looking into this "Jesus" thing. Quite honestly, I only started to show interest in that area because of a girl. That girl ended up being my wife, so God must of known what He was doing to get my attention. Eventually, after studying and understanding the Bible teachings more, I decided to place my faith in Jesus. So I did what I thought I was supposed to do. I said the sinners prayer and accepted Christ. A few days later I thought maybe I did it wrong because I was still sinning. So, I said the prayer again only this time with more emphasis. Boy, did I have a lot to learn about the Christian walk. It was only after I was married and attended other Bible studies, church teachings and marriage classes that I really began to understand who Jesus is and what He had done for me. I began to really understand and believe what I said I believed. I also got involved with youth groups and began doing lessons and working with young kids. There is a saying, "If you really want to learn something, teach it". That couldn't be more true for me. I directed and ran a week long Christian youth camp for several years. During that time, I believe I learned more about my faith than any other time in my life. When you are entrusted with teaching the minds of the next generation and shaping their beliefs, if forces you to take it very seriously and to learn all that you can to make sure you are speaking the truth. I have been fortunate to lead teachings in small group Bible studies as well as many Sunday sermons in our local church. Teaching really is a great way to learn and stay connected to His truths.

God continues to challenge me in many areas of my life. Like many believers, I struggle with giving up control of my life and trusting God to take care of things. I have fallen short many times in my life but God is faithful and continues to pursue me. There have been many times that I have seen God work in and through me. God is not a feeling but His presence in my life has been felt. One of those times was when I went on a mission trip to Mexico and saw God work in the hearts of those we served. I saw God in the eyes of the children and adults and watched their joy as they believed and accepted Jesus as their savior. I have seen God change the hearts of the hardest men and break them down in tears as they accepted Christ. I have experienced God's personal empowerment in my life while enduring personal tragedy with the loss of my youngest brother from a car accident. I believe one of the biggest tests to anyone's faith is losing a loved one. It was probably one of the most difficult times of my life, but I have seen God use that tragedy to bring others closer to Him. Trusting God does not make life easy but it does give you peace in the midst of the storm. I am thankful for His peace in times of great storms.

For me, God is strength. God is the still calm voice in times of chaos. He is eternal perspective and a solid foundation when the world around me is crumbling. God is comfort and peace of mind. He is forgiveness when I fall short and encouragement to keep moving forward. He is a provider of blessings and a protector of my mind, body and my soul. He is compassionate and a softener of hearts. He is confidence in a storm of self-doubt. God is truth in a world of lies. God is the director of my steps to accomplish His will and His purpose for me. I have experienced God's love and power first hand and I hope you do too. I hope that you trust Jesus and place your faith in Him alone and experience God for yourself.

Believe in Jesus

Everyone has beliefs. You may substitute the phrase "I believe" in front of anything and no one will question the validity of your belief. A belief means a person may accept or acknowledge something. To believe requires nothing of you. But what if that belief had consequences? What if your belief was going to cost you something? Would you still believe? Are you willing to put yourself at risk for what you believe? Do you have belief to the point of conviction? When you have belief with conviction that means you take a belief very seriously as if it is a reflection of yourself or part of your identity. A belief is something that you can change, a conviction is not.

I watched a lesson at a youth event several years ago that really stuck with me and illustrated belief to the point of conviction. My youth pastor asked me to go to the weight room and bench press as much as I could without letting any of the kids from the youth group see or know how much I had benched. When he began his lesson he asked the group if they believed that I bench pressed the amount of weight that was on the bar? Almost every hand went up in the air indicating that they believed that I could bench press the amount on the bar. He then asked them how many were willing to miss breakfast if they were wrong in their belief? Many hands that were up in the air came down. How many were willing to miss tomorrow's breakfast and lunch if they were wrong? Many more hands came down. He then asked, how many were willing to miss their next two meals and give up their shoes if they were wrong in their belief? All of the hands went down except for one person. One kids hand remained raised. So, the question is, how many of the kids really believed? One kid out of the thirty kids there truly believed what they said they believed. One person was willing to believe no matter what the cost. That is a lesson on belief to the point of conviction. Well, at the end of the lesson, all of the kids wanted to see if I could really bench press the weight on the bar that the pastor said I could lift. That is when the pastor gave a lesson on faith. He said, "Faith is believing in what you do not see. For you live by faith and not by sight". That lesson always stuck with me because it holds so true to your Christian walk.

Do you really believe what you say you believe? What you believe shapes who you are and what you do. Do you really believe Jesus is who He says He is? What are you willing to give up for that belief? If you really believe to the point of conviction, then would you risk embarrassment for His name, or risk ridicule by your peers or worse, give up your life in His name? What if you were faced with the question of choosing death or renouncing Jesus? Would you have the conviction of belief to maintain your loyalty and faith to Jesus? What are you willing to give up in His name?

Jesus is not a tool to fix your life. It does not mean that all the bad things in your life will go away. In fact, your life may get harder. This is the reality of following Christ. Jesus did not come to fix your life, He came to fix your relationship with God. Jesus' sole purpose was to fix your sin problem with God The penalty of Sin is death (eternal separation from God). Jesus came to redeem you back to God. To pay a penalty that He did not deserve, a debt that He did not create. Jesus Christ came to stand in your place to take your punishment of an eternity separated from God. He died, was buried and was resurrected and He will come back again. It is by believing in that alone that you are saved. It is your belief in Christ alone that saves you. It is Christ plus nothing. It is not Christ plus being religious or Christ plus doing good works or Christ plus going to church. It is about trusting and believing in Jesus Christ alone and becasue of that relationship you want to live a life that glorifies Him and love others so that they can know Him too.

It is so important that you understand who Jesus is and be convinced that He was who He said He was and did what He said He did. What you believe shapes who you are and what you do. You must examine the evidence. Your faith in Jesus is not a blind faith. You must look at the complexities of this world, study the Bible, listen to His teachings, look at the prophecies and make a decision based on what you truly believe. No one can make that decision for you. It is your decision to make. Do you believe in Jesus Christ to the point of conviction?

43050286R00071

Made in the USA
San Bernardino, CA
13 December 2016